W9-DJK-724

THE COMPLETE BOOK OF
BASKETRY
TECHNIQUES

THE COMPLETE BOOK OF
BASKETRY
TECHNIQUES

Sue Gabriel & Sally Goymer

A DAVID & CHARLES CRAFT BOOK
Newton Abbot · London

(*page 2*) Hedgerow basket made by Sheila Wynter using
commercial white willow and steamed black maul,
snowberry, maple, ivy, dogrose, rush, wisteria,
weeping willow, ornamental *Salix viminalis*
and ornamental *Salix alba* (*E. J. Wynter*)

TT
8 79
B3
G23
1991

British Library Cataloguing in Publication Data
Gabriel, Sue
The complete book of basketry techniques.
1. Basketry
I. Title   II. Goymer, Sally
746.412

ISBN 0-7153-9424-X

Text and illustrations © Sue Gabriel and Sally Goymer 1991

All rights reserved. No part of this publication may be reproduced,
stored in a retrieval system, or transmitted, in any form or by any
means, electronic, mechanical, photocopying, recording or otherwise,
without the prior permission of David & Charles plc

Typeset by ABM Typographics Ltd Hull
and printed in Hong Kong
by Wing King Tong Co Ltd
for David & Charles plc
Brunel House   Newton Abbot   Devon

Distributed in the United States by
Sterling Publishing Co. Inc.
387 Park Avenue South, New York, NY 10016-8810

3 3001 00776 3989

CONTENTS

INTRODUCTION

Our aims in writing this book are twofold. Firstly, there is a need for a good straightforward practical book on techniques, methods and design of basketry, for existing and aspiring basket-makers. Secondly, with the current interest and pride in traditional rural crafts, people who love the craft should have access to realistic information about the basketry trade in order to promote quality and encourage raised standards, for the benefit of both makers and users.

Good craftsmanship is a difficult commodity to define, but it involves skill and experience, truth to materials, and a non-compromising attitude to quality. Aesthetics become an integral part of the total process. Such criteria can only apply when an article is made entirely by hand.

Basketry can appear mundane because of its essentially utilitarian nature, and because it continues. It has not become special by being lost to present-day society. Despite this, basketry is one of our oldest crafts, predating even pottery. It utilises natural indigenous materials which can be used with very little processing and preparation.

Various techniques and methods have been developed specific to local materials, giving rise to an enormous variety of styles and traditions. For this reason, basketry worldwide is richly varied, even within different regions of the same country. The study of regional baskets in relation to history and local culture is fascinating in itself.

Initially, early baskets were probably little more than a tangled mass of twigs, gradually developing into a woven form, for greater stability and a longer life. Once a basic structural technique had evolved, basketry became a vital craft to any society. Before the advent of modern materials, baskets were a light and cheap container to make.

Baskets have been used for every conceivable purpose; as containers for gathering and storing, for carrying and hauling, for living in and sitting on, for travelling in and with, and for holding food – and even water. Basketwork has produced fencing and fish traps, huts and hats, chariots, chairs and clothing, animal muzzles and cages, cradles and coffins. Baskets have been disposable or durable, rough and ready, or of such fine quality as to be extremely valuable. They can be large, rough and robust, or fragile and delicate, decorative or simple in concept, light and airy, or close woven and solid.

The materials needed for basket-making were eventually grown as a cash-crop to supply the expanding trade. References to willow growing date from the twelfth century, increasing in suitable areas until the decline towards the end of the nineteenth century. Throughout the centuries, basketry has remained a hand-

Hawker's basket, as used by London street flower-sellers (*Institute of Agricultural History and Museum of English Rural Life, University of Reading*)

made craft. It has never been mechanised, owing to the irregular nature of the material, although it has supplied industry with standardised examples of the craft, for example, the herring cran which had to be made to exact specifications as it was an official measure.

The development of technology in various fields has meant a decline in the everyday use of basketry. Packaging is now largely made of paper, card or plastic. Carrier bags have replaced shopping baskets. In almost every field there is a modern equivalent to preclude the use of a basket.

In addition to this, the importing of baskets from countries where labour is cheap has fuelled the decline of basket-making in the West. There are fewer and fewer skilled basketmakers to pass on the techniques to future generations. The apprenticeship system has gone, and few people have been prepared to put in the years of hard work required to build up expertise. The only basketmakers continuing to develop the craft in Britain were the blind, working with purely tactile considerations.

The society that invented built-in

An assortment of modern packaging

obsolescence and the disposable culture has no place for a piece of craftsmanship using natural living materials which could last a lifetime. One notable exception to this has been the balloon basket. The combined qualities of lightness, strength and resilience make basketwork the most suitable method of construction.

The inevitable backlash has meant that a resurgence of interest in natural crafts has recently brought basketry into greater prominence. Artists and craftspeople from other disciplines have moved into the craft, bringing new research and developments. Amateur and professional craftspeople are beginning to get together to pool their knowledge and experience to keep the craft alive. The Basketmakers Association has done much to promote awareness of the craft and to revive old traditions before it is too late, as well as support future development.

For anyone who is interested in taking up the craft of basketmaking, time spent watching and learning from someone who has already mastered the techniques is essential. If you have skills in another craft involving nimble fingers, strong hands and an eye for form, texture or structure, these will all help. The stronger you are, the larger the baskets you will be able to make, but there are types of basketmaking which do not require strength so much as control. Provided that you take your time and persevere in developing your skills, tackling techniques that are within your range, you should produce good results. The difficult things take years of practice, so don't be tempted to sacrifice quality for speed. Be prepared to expend the time and effort required for the more complex techniques.

We intend that this book will be used as a guide for beginners, for whom the Programme of Work (Chapter 10) was specifically designed, as well as a reference manual for more experienced basketmakers. We have covered basic and more advanced techniques, with the emphasis on willow work, and advice based on our own experiences. Like any craft worth learning, the more you learn the more you realise there is to learn. We hope that this book will encourage many more basketmakers, users and collectors to further their interest in this absorbing craft.

Chapter 1
MATERIALS

Baskets have been made everywhere in the world and their style, design and shape are largely determined by the materials that grow locally. In tropical climates, where palms and grasses are abundant, they are plaited, coiled or woven. In the Far East, Japan and China, bamboo and cane are the principal materials. They are used whole or split to make harder, more rigid baskets.

Devon splint baskets by George Trickery (*Institute of Agricultural History and Museum of English Rural Life, University of Reading*)

In Britain and northern Europe, willow has become the traditional material, woven in the stake-and-strand method to produce wicker work. Other traditional materials are various woods cleaved into splints for frame and slatted baskets, and rushes which can be coiled or woven into softer baskets. The range of materials from which baskets can and have been made is enormously wide; from pine needles to oak trees, newspaper to telephone wire. Crossing the barriers from natural to man-made materials, there is tremendous scope for ingenuity.

The most commonly used natural materials are now used commercially. The most suitable varieties are grown, harvested and prepared for sale, saving the basketmaker a great deal of time and trouble. Both indigenous and imported materials are readily available. The following is a brief summary of the processes involved in their cultivation.

RUSH

Scirpus lacustris is the variety mainly used for both basketry and chair seating. It has a tall, unjointed, bright-green stem with a cluster of small brown flowers near the top. The height, 4-10ft (120-300cm), and the colour vary, depending on the conditions. It grows best in slow moving rivers and streams, being cut

Baskets from around the world using indigenous materials

every other July, as near the root as possible. This is done with a sharp billhook, by either wading into the water or leaning out of a boat. The smaller rush, *Juncus effusis,* can be used in exactly the same way but for much finer work.

After harvesting, the rushes are laid out to dry, under cover if the weather is wet. This can take several weeks, as they need turning every so often to avoid any damp patches which would encourage mould. They are then stored flat in a dry, dark place to retain their colour.

Before using, the rushes must be graded into small, medium and thick. To prepare for use, immerse them in water for a few minutes or lay them on the ground and hose down. Once dampened, they must be wrapped for a while, most conveniently overnight, to mellow.

STRAW

The use of straw in basketry is mainly confined to plaiting strips, which are then sewn together for hats and light baskets, or coiling techniques, as in the old-fashioned bee skeps. Any of the cereal crops can be used, the longer the distance between ear and first joint the better.

Cutting by hand or binder is essential, as combine harvesting destroys the straw. It is cut just before it is ripe, trimmed above the first joint, stripped of leaves, graded, tied into small bundles and left to dry. It must be stored flat out of the reach of mice (a second-hand tin trunk is ideal).

To prepare for use, bunch the required amount with an elastic band near the base of the bundle. Turn the bundle upside down and insert a knitting needle (or similar) under the band. Hold by the needle and pour boiling water down the stems. Use immediately. (Soaking in cold water takes much longer and discolours the straw.)

RAFFIA

Raffia comes from an imported palm leaf from Madagascar. It can be bought in most craft shops and garden centres and is easily dyed. It is used mainly for coiled work, either stitched over coils of raffia or using another core such as cane or rope. No preparation is needed unless the raffia is particularly brittle, in which case it can be dipped in warm water.

CANE

Cane is imported from South East Asia, mostly Indonesia. The heavier ones such as tohiti and malacca are for furniture making and walking sticks. Kubu and palembang, being more flexible, are used in industrial basketmaking. Sarawak and Segah supply the rattan for centre cane and chair seating.

Rattan or whole cane is a creeper with a thorny bark which grows in the jungle. The outer thorny layer is removed on site to reveal a shiny inner bark. This is then stripped by machine into widths of 0-6mm for chair seating. The inner pith is then divided by machine into various diameters, cane sizes 000-20 (1-12mm) for basketmaking. It is also machined into flat oval lapping and flat band cane. Cane should be stored in a cool dry place. Too much warmth makes it brittle.

Rush basketmaking (*Institute of Agricultural History and Museum of English Rural Life, Reading*)

Mr Hill of Camelsdale at work making bee skeps (*Institute of Agricultural History and Museum of English Rural Life, Reading*)

WILLOW

The willow-growing industry is centred in and around the Somerset Levels, where the majority of the willow crop is *Salix triandra,* 'Black Maul'.

Growth and Harvesting

A withy bed is planted by pushing 9-12in (22-30cm) lengths (cut from the butt ends of stout rods) into the prepared ground about 14in (35cm) apart. The distance between rows is about 27in (68cm) to accommodate the harvesting machines which are now widely used in place of the traditional billhook. For the first few years the harvest is small, and keeping the beds free of weeds is as important as pest control. Each year in winter, when the sap is down, the rods are cut level with the ground which

(*above*) Raffia woven onto a wire frame

(*right*) Assortment of baskets made with centre cane

encourages more growth the following year. After three years or so, the density of growth inhibits weeds and leaf fall forms a natural compost. The dangers of a ruined crop are not over; late frost can damage growing tips and cause them to fork, so cattle are grazed in the beds to eat the new shoots which will grow again.

In the past, most villages had their own basketmaker whose willows were grown alongside streams and riverbanks and along ditches dividing fields. Although long neglected, these willows can be recognised by the trunk about shoulder height and the bulbous shape at the point where the rods shoot out (now mostly left to grow into large branches). They were cut at this height to prevent the cattle devouring the crop.

Preparation for Sale

After harvesting, the rods are sorted into sizes according to their height. This is still done by the traditional method on most farms. A large oil drum with a measuring stick attached to the side is sunk into the ground. Bundles of willow are dropped in. Everything over 7ft (210cm) is removed by taking hold of the top handful and shaking it clear of all the smaller lengths. This is repeated at 6ft (180cm), and so on. Any damaged material is removed at this point.

At this stage the rods are called 'green'. The proportion of the crop to be left with

(*far left*) Grading willows for length (*Institute of Agricultural History and Museum of English Rural Life, Reading*)

(*left*) Stripping willows with a brake (*Institute of Agricultural History and Museum of English Rural Life, Reading*)

(*below left*) Solid-fuel boiler for buffing willows (*Institute of Agricultural History and Museum of English Rural Life, Reading*)

(*below*) Stripping willows by machine (*Institute of Agricultural History and Museum of English Rural Life, Reading*)

Willow beds in full growth
(*Sally Goymer*)

Pitted willows in full leaf
(*Sally Goymer*)

the bark on will be allowed to dry naturally and will then be called 'brown' although this does not necessarily correspond with the actual colour, which will vary according to the species, soil and weather conditions. When the bark is stripped from the rods it reveals a creamy white colour which is much prized now since it is becoming more and more difficult to obtain.

To obtain 'white' willow, the cut bundles are stood in several inches of water to keep them alive, preferably with their butt ends hidden from light to inhibit root growth. When the sap has risen and they have grown into full leaf the following spring the bark loosens prior to the growth of new branches, at which point the bark can be more easily removed. Stripping was once done entirely by hand on a metal brake rather like a large old fashioned dolly peg; however it is now done by machine, feeding handfuls of rods at a time into a rotating drum covered in small versions of the old style brake. It is also possible to leave the rods uncut until spring, when they must be stripped within a week of cutting before they dry out.

'Buff' willow is obtained by boiling the cut bundles (still with the bark on) for 8-10 hours. This has the double effect of making it much easier to strip and of staining the rods. The colour comes from tannin in the bark which also helps to preserve the wood. This method can be used at any time in the year although winter buffing creates a darker shade than the golden colour obtained in the summer. The rods are stripped straight from the tank while still warm. After stripping, buff and white rods are stood to dry, tied to fences to keep them upright.

After drying, the rods are tied into 'bolts' with a twisted rod, approximately 36in (92cm) in circumference, just above the base. The price varies according to colour, irrespective of the height range of 3-8ft (90-240cm). The rods in any bundle will be no taller than the sold height but will range down to the height sold below. It is also possible to buy bundles of thick sticks for using as handles and for corner posts in square work. Some suppliers will sell bundles of mixed sizes, which are useful for beginners.

Good willow should be smooth, without blemish or scab; the tips should be fine and straight with as little pith as possible. In large quantities it is stored on its side, stacked tip to butt, but the average worker will want to store it on its butt ends.

HEDGEROW WOODS

A wide range of other woods can be used with the same techniques as for willow. Hedgerow materials are free and easily available, although it is necessary beforehand to obtain permission from the owner of a particular hedge. There is a tremendous range of colours and textures available although they will fade and shrink to a certain extent, requiring additional material to be woven in to fill the gaps. The use of hedgerow in commercial work is limited as the quality and availability of the material cannot be guaranteed from year to year.

Both leafy and woody varieties can be used. Leaves are treated like rush. Certain species are known to work well but it is worth experimenting with anything which looks suitable. Look for long pliable rods or stems which are cut in winter when the sap is down, after the leaves have fallen and before the new growth appears in the spring. Stuff needs to be tied into bundles according to type and size and left partially to dry. The idea is for the wood to do the maximum amount of shrinking without drying out and becoming brittle. Drying time will depend on weather conditions but is generally between one and three months. Drying is best done outdoors to avoid causing too-rapid shrinkage which can damage the bark: under a hedge where it is partially protected is appropriate. Hedgerow material which has dried out too much can sometimes be soaked down like commercial willow, but this is not often successful as the wood deteriorates and the bark cracks.

Suggested Varieties

Sticks/Stakes
Willows
Dogwood
Privet
Larch
Sweet Chestnut

Weaving
Willows
Broom
Jasmine
Periwinkle
Elm and Lime suckers
Ivy
Clematis
Honeysuckle
Wild Rose
Blackthorn

Manufactured Materials

This group includes man-made materials
such as plastic raffia and cord, as well as
natural materials such as wool and sea-
grass, which are processed before they
can be used. In addition to this, many
basketmakers are now using basketry
techniques with other materials such as
wire, different types of plastic, paper,
card and a variety of yarns and fibres. To
use such an assortment of materials
effectively demands considerable knowledge of a range of suitable techniques.
However, time and trouble can be re-
warded with exciting and innovative
results, capable of extending the craft
beyond the bounds of tradition.

Bolts of willow: buff, white, steamed and
brown

Chapter 2
WORKSHOP, TOOLS AND EQUIPMENT

Theoretically, baskets can be made without the use of any tools. Tools are used to make the work easier and the finished article neater. Basketry is not a mechanised craft: what machinery there is is used in the harvesting and preparation of the raw material. The basic tools required are a knife to cut the material, a bodkin to open up the weave and a rapping iron to close it down. Many of the tools are easily available or improvised. Those that are not can be obtained from specialist suppliers. Not all the tools listed below are used in all techniques or for all materials. Specific uses will be explained in the chapters on techniques.

BASIC TOOLS

Bodkin

A steel spike with a handle, used where a rod has to be pushed through or into the work. It is available in a range of sizes depending on the size of the work. Most craftsmen will only need one or two.

Shears

These are similar to secateurs, which can also be used for the same purpose.

They are useful for trimming the finished work and cutting sticks.

Knife

Necessary for slyping, scalloming and other types of cutting.

Rapping Iron

A heavy, blunt-edged tool for knocking down the weave.

Grease Horn

This need not be a horn. It should be a heavy unbreakable container which can store the bodkins when not in use or a short length of pipe, blocked at one end. The grease used is tallow mixed with plumber's hemp. The hemp prevents too much grease adhering to the bodkin. The thin film which remains lubricates the bodkin and makes it easier to use. (If tallow is not available, substitute lard.)

Weights

Weights are used to stabilise the work in progress. When working on a lap board it will be necessary to skewer the weight to the board.

Basic tools

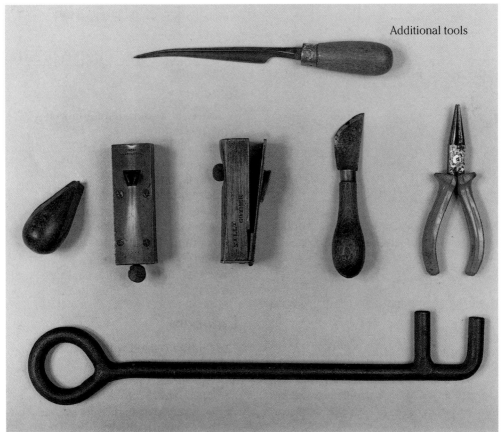

Additional tools

Measure

A rigid rule can easily be made and marked in inches or centimetres. It will need to be at least 2ft (60cm) long. A folding yard or metre stick is a good alternative and for larger work, a flexible steel rule is useful.

Screwblock

A wooden clamp with metal wing nuts, ideally 2ft (60cm) long, 6in (15cm) deep and 2½in (6cm) high. It is used for holding the sticks rigid when bases or lids are being woven for square work.

ADDITIONAL TOOLS

Cleave

A wooden tool, sometimes metal tipped, used for splitting rods into three or four from tip to butt.

Shave

Used on split lengths of willow, it works in a similar fashion to a carpenter's plane, shaving the pith from the skein to the thickness required.

Upright

A tool used to shave the skein to a uniform width for fine work.

Picking Knife

A traditional tool used to 'pick' off untidy ends. Now largely replaced by shears.

Shell Bodkin

Useful for easing rods through in awkward places.

Commander

This is usually a ring in the top end of a rapping iron and it is used to straighten bent sticks. For large work a 'dog' iron would be used.

Round-nosed Pliers

Used specifically for canework to squeeze the fibres in order that the material may be bent at an acute angle without cracking.

WORKING METHODS

Baskets can be made sitting on the floor, standing up or anywhere in between. Traditionally, work is done with the craftsman seated close to the ground. Bases can be made in a variety of ways depending on the shape and size, and the convenience to the craftsman. Round and oval bases can be made under foot or knee using bodyweight to aid control. For small work they can be made on the lap or against the body. Square bases can be made by clamping the base sticks into a screwblock or by clamping them to the workbench using bodyweight to hold them in position. After staking up, the basket is usually completed in front of the craftsman on a lapboard or table.

WORKSHOP EQUIPMENT

Benches

A convenient and adaptable system for working requires two benches, one 12in (30cm) high and one 8in (20cm) high. This gives a combination of three working levels, a third height of 20in (50cm) being obtained by standing one on top of the other. The lowest height bench needs to be large enough in surface area safely to accommodate the other bench on top. A lip along the back and one side of the lower bench helps to prevent the top one slipping.

Lapboard

The lapboard used with the bench is approximately 20in (50cm) by 28in (70cm), the legs are 2in (5cm) higher at the working end. There are a series of holes drilled every two inches from the working end towards the middle. These are

Using a bench and lap board

Working a base under foot and on the plank (*Institute of Agricultural History and Museum of English Rural Life, University of Reading*)

used to skewer the base of a basket to the lapboard, with the aid of a bodkin or similar spike, in a convenient working position. Many basketmakers prefer to sit on a raised plank with a simple lapboard with a ledge under one end.

Moulds

A mould is a wooden former around which a basket is made. It can be solid or in sections and is used for making a series of uniform baskets or for complex shapes. Where the top of the basket is smaller than the base or sides, it needs to be in sections in order to be removable. Moulds are rarely seen in Britain but are widely used in Europe and the Far East where mass production is more common.

Hoops and Formers

Hoops are used outside the stakes once they have been upsett to hold them upright. They can also be used inside to determine the upper diameter. They are generally made of some lightweight material, such as cane or willow. In fitched work, metal hoops and formers can be used inside to keep the shape rigid until the waling and border are finished. On squarework with corner posts a frame can be used to keep the posts at right angles. With blunt corners two sticks of equal length can be wedged diagonally inside the basket. Wooden formers are also used to shape the whole or split rods for framework baskets.

Tanks

A professional basketmaker would need to have a tank at least 6ft (2m) long, 2ft

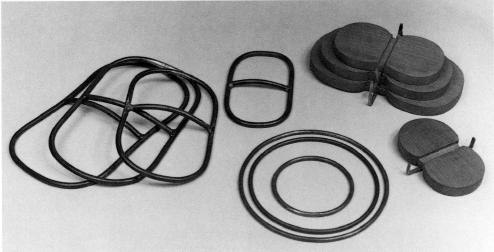

(*top*) Sectional fishing creel mould, simple round and oval solid moulds

(*above*) Hoops and formers

(60cm) wide and 2ft (60cm) high with a water supply and a means of draining. In practice a tank can be any water container big enough to take the material to be soaked, from a plant trough to a domestic bath. A stream or a garden pond can be used but a galvanised tin bath in the garden is an ideal solution. Whichever method is used, the material must be submerged. An easy way to achieve this is to put a short piece of plank weighted down with bricks, across each end of the water.

Soaking tank showing cross sections to keep material submerged

Sulphur

The purpose of a sulphur room is to destroy any mould forming on damp willows. A side effect of the process is a mild bleaching which improves the appearance of white willow. In large workshops a sulphur room can be the size of a small garage, but for the individual a large box or plastic dustbin sufficient to take several baskets will do. Wet the baskets before putting them inside. Place a small bowl with approximately one tablespoon (1 x 15ml spoon) of sulphur powder at floor level and ignite. The door or lid of the container must be close fitting, but not airtight. Leave for a minimum of two hours, or for preference overnight. The burning sulphur gives off a gas that combines with the water on the baskets to produce a mild acid. Any metal in contact with the willow during the process (ie nails) will discolour the immediate area.

Note
The sulphur room should be outside the house as the fumes are extremely unpleasant. Children and pets should be kept away.

Oxalic Acid

A similar effect can be obtained with oxalic acid. Dissolve a commercial pack in a dustbin-sized container of water. Stir until the liquid is milky white. Plunge the basket in for a few moments. Drain the excess water off into the lid of the dustbin and pour back into the container. This liquid will keep for six months.

Chapter 3

STRUCTURES

There are an enormous number of variations on the ways that baskets can be constructed depending on the materials used, regional specialities and individual innovations. The following is an explanation of some of the basic types of structure.

STAKE-AND-STRAND

The stake-and-strand method of basketmaking is a very versatile method using flexible weavers to work round rigid stakes.

Baskets made in this way are usually constructed by first making a round, oval or rectangular base. The stakes, which will give the basket its strength, are inserted into the base by various methods and then turned upwards to form the structure on which the sides are woven. The ends of these stakes are then worked down into a strong border. Lids, partitions, handles etc can be incorporated into an enormous variety of shapes and sizes of baskets.

Most of the techniques used in this method have been designed to accommodate indigenous materials, commonly the supple young branches of native trees, in particular those of the genus *Salix* (willow). The qualities of suppleness and strength, as well as the range of lengths and thicknesses, have enabled the basketmaker to develop those weaves which best suit the various parts of a basket, turning to advantage the tapering lengths so that the woven basket becomes an integrated whole. Although other materials such as centre cane are often used, the stake-and-strand technique is best suited to those materials for which it evolved. The great variety of willow species and the various methods of preparation allow inventive patterning, using colour variation in conjunction with differing textures of the weaves.

The scope for design using shape, texture and colour within the natural behaviour of a living material is infinite. It is possible to make baskets to specific sizes and for specific purposes as well as freer structures. The many thousands of designs already in existence owe credit to the inventiveness and skills of generations of basketmakers.

FRAME OR RIBBED

This method also uses flexible weavers woven around rigid stakes, but in this case the basic shape of the basket is first constructed using a rigid framework of ribs. Often these ribs have been pre-shaped around moulds or formers.

In general this method has been used by skillful amateurs rather than professional basketmakers. The various styles and techniques have been localised and

(*left*) Traditional stake-and-strand oval shopping basket

have become regional traditions, particularly among the Celtic communities and in rural areas. They are also common in the US, many styles having evolved from their British ancestors.

The materials used for the framework can be split willow rods or wide splints of ash, oak or hazel. There are various methods of making and holding the structure together, although the weaving is usually randing, using splints, split rods or fine lengths of willow or hazel. In

(*above*) Irish potato basket by Alison Fitzgerald; frame shopping basket copied from an original design by Mr D. J. Davies; melon basket in centre cane

some cases green (fresh cut) material can be used.

Although the freedom of design is constrained by the limitations of the basic structure, a huge variety of traditional methods has evolved in different areas. The resulting baskets are strong, serviceable and pleasing to hand and eye.

PLAITED

Plaited basketry uses flat strands of material of even width. This is a versatile technique although it usually results in fairly lightweight, decorative baskets unsuitable for heavy work. There is great scope for working out patterns simply and cheaply with strips of coloured paper, and indeed baskets themselves can be made very successfully in this way. Interlacing and overlay techniques can together create multi-directional patterns.

It is possible to weave a wide range of basket shapes by working over moulds. Mats can be woven either as a complete shape or by joining woven strips together. These methods are commonly seen in rushwork, and also plaited straw which once was the basis for a large industry.

COILED

Coiled baskets are constructed on a central core, which is stitched with finer, more pliable material. The central core can be either solid, such as centre cane (known in the US as reed), or bunches of softer material worked together, such as straw. The stitching can be merely sufficient to hold each succeeding ring of the spiralling core together or it may totally cover the core.

There are many varied styles using this technique, from the fine, intricate decorative work of the American Indians to the larger, more solid straw constructions which have developed in Britain to make log baskets, chairs and bee skeps. There are also baskets made by coiling plaits or braids made from various materials and stitching the coils together.

Most baskets worked in this essentially spiral technique are round or oval, the shape being limited to the possibilities afforded by a widening or narrowing coil. However the scope for pattern and elaborate stitching is infinite. Many types of thread could be used in an endless combination of colour and pattern to incorporate beautiful designs into an essentially simple structure.

TWINED

This technique is perhaps closest to those used in fabric weaving and generally uses fairly soft materials. The weave consists of a 'weft' of two weavers which work together around each 'warp' strand, crossing over each other in between.

Very often the twining 'wefts' completely cover the 'warps' although a lace-like effect can be produced by leaving spaces between each row of weaving.

These ways of using a twisting pair of weavers are also used in the stake-and-strand technique, where it is called 'pairing' and 'fitching'. The twining technique is also often seen in rushwork in conjunction with other weaves. Since this

Coiled baskets using a variety of stitches

(*opposite page above*) Plaited rush baskets (*below*) Examples of twined basketry

'Oriole pocket' by Linda Lugenbill (centre cane and striped honeysuckle vine) (*Linda Lugenbill*)

method often involves working with fairly soft materials, the shaping is usually done over moulds. The resulting 'fabric' can be very hard wearing.

Patterning is produced both by variations in the weave and use of colour. Many of the suitable fibres are indigenous to warmer climates. One of these is sisal, which takes dye extremely well and can produce intricate colour patterning.

CONTEMPORARY BASKETS

Although this is not a single structural technique, the term arises because there are being produced today many articles, both functional and sculptural, which use basketwork materials or techniques, either alone or with other skills.

Since many traditional uses for baskets have been superseded, some workers feel that the rapport they have with these traditional skills can be utilised in other ways. Sculptors and textile designers look towards the materials and methods traditional to the basketmaker. Other materials such as paper, metals and plastics are also being explored in relation to basketry techniques to produce works which may be functional or of purely visual or tactile interest.

As a result of this diverse experimentation the differences between textiles, basketry and sculpture are becoming blurred and indefinable. The term 'art' or 'contemporary' basketry is now commonly used to describe this area.

FURNITURE

Strictly speaking, furniture which is entirely or partly made with basketry materials or techniques, being a vast subject in itself, is not within the scope of this book. However, as it is a significant part of the basketry trade it deserves a mention.

The most common item of furniture using basketry is the chair. Since the days of ancient Egypt and Rome, local basketry materials have been used to make cheap, light and comfortable seating.

Chairs have been made using coiling and stake-and-strand. Techniques have also been developed to incorporate woven backs and seats into wooden frames. These include rush, cane, whole and skeined willow and splints. With the solid wood frame for strength, the chair maker has had greater scope for design and innovation, sometimes using very fine materials.

(*left*) Child's high chair by Sheila Wynter

Chapter 4
BASICS AND SPECIAL TECHNIQUES

WORKING WITH CENTRE CANE

Centre-cane techniques have evolved from willow techniques, but, although the weaves may be the same, it is important to appreciate the differences. Its suppleness makes it easier for beginners to handle but the most obvious feature is that cane comes in uniform widths and much greater lengths. Sizes chosen must be appropriate for the basket and weavers must always be finer than stakes. Centre cane is also unsuitable for very large items as it lacks rigidity, although this is compensated for to a certain extent by the use of bye stakes to strengthen the siding. It is very supple and versatile, the continuous lengths requiring less complex methods to avoid joins. This quality lends itself particularly well to decorative treatment such as dyeing and the use of fancy variations on basic weaves.

To prepare for working, soak the cane in hot water for two to ten minutes, depending on the size. If using cold water, the cane will require slightly longer soaking. The cane is ready to use immediately, but it sometimes helps to mellow it for about ten minutes under a damp cloth.

WORKING WITH WILLOW

As willow is a natural material, the range of sizes within a bolt will vary considerably. It cannot be emphasised enough that the more accurate the sorting the better the basket. Ideally, as each new bolt is opened it should be sorted into sizes. Sit with the bolt between the legs taking handfuls at a time, putting thick to one side and thin to the other. Repeat with each bundle, to make four bundles altogether.

When choosing rods to work with, consider the thickness at the point where the rods will be used for the border of the basket. If possible refer to another basket of equivalent size as it can be very easy to misjudge sizes in the bolt. As a very general guide, use 3ft (90cm) for fine small baskets, 4ft (120cm), 5ft (150cm) and 6ft (180cm) for shopping baskets, 7ft (210cm), and 8ft (240cm) for large items including log baskets.

Soaking times will vary according to the type of willow, the size and the temperature. Buff can be soaked for as little as thirty minutes or up to two hours. Although it can be used for weaving immediately it benefits from mellowing. Wrap in well wrung-out sacking or other

Position of hands for normal weaving

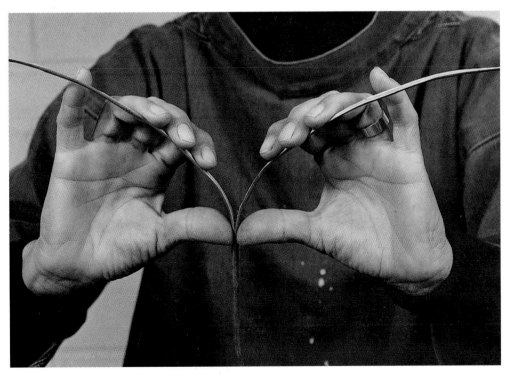

Splitting a willow rod in two

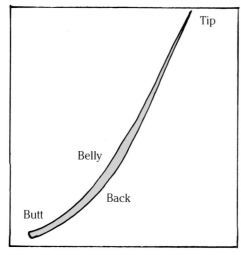

1 Structure of a willow rod

cloth (not soaking wet) or plastic sheeting and leave for at least as long as the soaking time or, if more convenient, overnight. White willow takes slightly longer than buff to soak. Brown willow takes at least two days and up to a week in winter for the larger sizes.

Although willow does not bend continuously, it is surprisingly supple, requiring positive treatment to ensure that kinks occur in appropriate places as the rod is woven. Control is maintained mainly with the left hand, using the thumb to hold the weaver in the correct position in front of each stake, while the right hand takes the weaver around the next one. Many of the techniques used

2a Slype

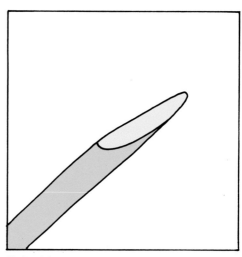

2b Straight cut

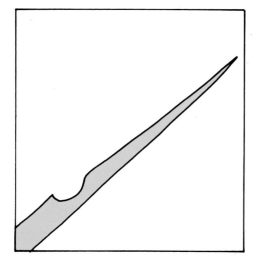

2c Scallom

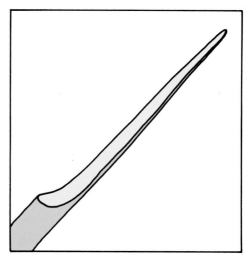

2d Shaved scallom

take account of the natural shape of a willow rod. There is a gentle curve from the butt end to the tip, and the degree of taper and the thickness of each rod vary a great deal (Fig 1). According to the particular technique being used, there are various ways of cutting the butt end of a willow rod (Fig 2).

Split Willow

Splitting rods into two or three makes a bolt go a great deal further and can be useful to reduce the soaking time for brown willow. The split rods lack strength but are useful for randing. They are both harder on the hands and awkward to work with.

Splitting a Rod into Two

1 Use dry rods.
2 Hold the butt end under one arm and split the tip with a knife.
3 With thumbs pointing towards you, ease the split gently along the rod.
4 If the split veers to one side, pull slightly more on the other side.

Using a Cleave

Three-or four-way cleaves are available.

1 Make a straight cut at the tip end of the rod, and pull back the end of the cut (Fig 3a).
2 Insert the cleave into the opening in the central pith and ease gently along the length of the rod (Fig 3b).
3 It is also possible to obtain a metal-tipped cleave which avoids the necessity of starting the split as above. Just insert the cleave into the tip end as before.

Making Skeins

To make skeins, two specialist tools are required: a shave and an upright.

1 First, split the rods by one of the methods outlined above.
2 Adjust the blade on the shave to a sufficient gap to accommodate the split rod.
3 Hold the rod in position under the blade with the left thumb, pith upwards, and pull through from tip to butt.
4 Adjust the screw to make a narrower gap and repeat until the desired thickness is achieved.
5 It is also possible to remove the pith by using a knife, but it is not possible to achieve such even thickness.
6 If skeins are required to be even width as well as thickness, then an upright is needed.
7 Set the blades to the required distance apart and pull the skein through from tip to butt with the skin facing upwards.

3a Preparing the tip end to insert the cleave

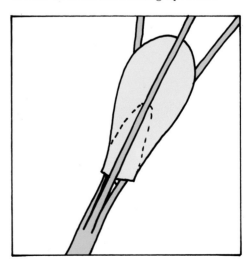

3b Using the cleave

Twisting a willow rod

Making a Twist

This technique breaks the skin of the rod and twists it tightly into a rope so it becomes both completely pliable and very strong. It can be problematical to learn, but practice on spare rods, and a little perseverance, should enable you to acquire the necessary skill. Once learned, it is extremely quick and simple to do. It is used for handles, hinges and some other wrapped techniques.

1 Secure the butt end.
2 Form the top 6in (15cm) or so of the tip end into the shape of a crank.
3 Twist the rod by winding as if it were a handle with the right hand.
4 Move the left hand gradually down the rod as each section becomes twisted.
5 When using the rod, retwist each section as needed, working from the butt end, keeping the twist secure and firm by ensuring that the twist is always under tension. Take care to twist enough to avoid splits showing but without over-twisting, which will mangle the rod.

USING MOULDS

The following instructions explain how to work a basket on a wooden mould.

1 Make the base to fit the mould and trim the sticks.
2 Position the base onto the bottom of the mould. Place at least two short pieces of mellowed willow across the weaving. Nail through these pegs, between the weaving and into the base of the mould.
3 Stake up so that the natural curve of the rods follows the line of the mould. Tie the stakes so that they lie close to the mould.
4 With the mould held between the knees, work the upsett in the normal way. As you work round each stake, pull it slightly away from the mould, ensuring that it is pushed back firmly into place after each stroke.
5 Continue weaving until the shape is complete, then untie the stakes.
6 Complete the basket, level with the top of the mould. Remove nails and pegs from the base, hold the mould by the handle and tap around the border with a rapping iron to release it.

Chapter 5
BASES
AND STAKING UP

The base is an important part of the basket. It forms the foundation for the rest of the structure. It must be firm and evenly woven, to give both strength and stability. Not only will an uneven base stop the basket from standing up properly, it will make the sides much more difficult to weave. It is worth taking time and trouble to get the base right before starting the sides.

There are various bases for different purposes as well as a variety of techniques for different shapes. Often, differences of technique have evolved as regional variations, building on local tradition. Both the structure and the working method may differ from one region to another.

While experimenting with techniques, it is possible to make a selection of bases and let the baskets evolve from them. However when the basket is to take a specific form, the whole basket must be considered before beginning the base as that form may determine the type of base needed. Specific base measurements and arrangements of sticks will be required to achieve a particular size and shape for the finished basket.

Due consideration must also be given to staking up the basket so that the siding is firmly and evenly attached to form an integrated structure. This will give the basket its strength and durability as well as visual impact.

ROUND BASES
Making a Slath

The number of sticks in the base is determined by the number of stakes required to work the border. This will depend on both the thickness of the stakes and the size of the basket. Fine stakes on a small basket can be as close as ½in (1cm), whereas on a log basket they could be up to 2in (5cm) apart. If the stakes are too close the basket will be difficult to weave, whereas if they are too widely spaced the basket will be weak. If in doubt try to copy the distance on another basket.

1 Having decided on a suitable number of stakes for the border, divide by four to give the number of sticks required for the base.
2 Cut sticks from the butt end of several stout rods; the thickness needs to be appropriate to the size of the basket. The minimum possible number is five and the maximum is twelve. They need to be cut the length of the diameter of the base plus an inch or so to allow for wastage.
3 The structure can be formed in two ways. First alternate the sticks tips and butts, then either pierce and thread them through (Fig 4a,b) or overlay them (Fig 4c).

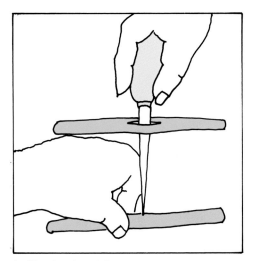

4a Piercing the sticks

4b Sticks threaded through

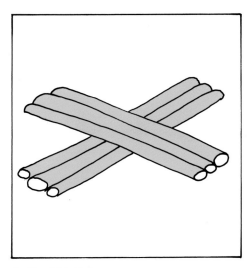

4c Overlaid sticks

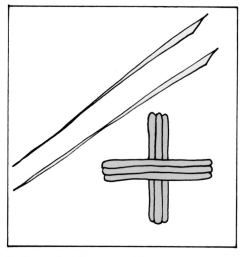

5a Crossed sticks and straight-cut weavers

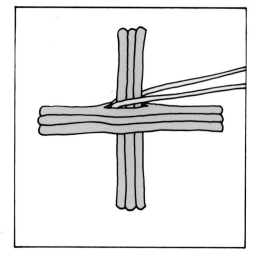

5b Beginning to weave

6 Alternative beginning

7 Canework beginning

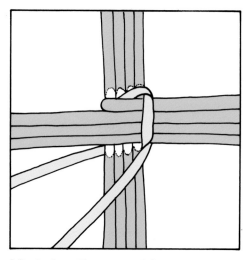

8 Beginning with an extra stick

Beginning the Base Weaving (tying in the slath)

There are several methods which can be used to begin the weaving as follows:

a) Starting with butt ends. Make a straight cut on the butt ends of two slender rods, and insert them into the left-hand side of the split (Fig 5 a,b).

b) Also starting with butts, but this time insert them into the split back to back so that they will weave over themselves. This is sometimes easier for beginners to control (Fig 6).

c) Starting with tip ends. This is done as

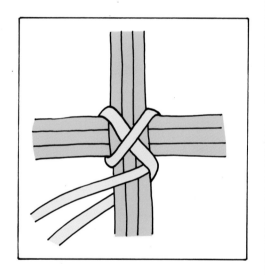

9 Decorative variations

the first method but is only used on very fine work.

d) Looped method. This is used in canework. Fold over a continuous length to start. Either squeeze at the point of bend with round-nosed pliers or make a firm twist in order to separate the fibres so that they do not crack (Fig 7).

e) Adding an extra stick. The sticks must be overlaid, not pierced. They can be shaved at the centre to make the base less bulky. The extra stick needs to be the same thickness as the other weaver, excluding the butt (Fig 8).

f) It is also possible to make many decorative variations at the centre, especially when using centre cane (Fig 9).

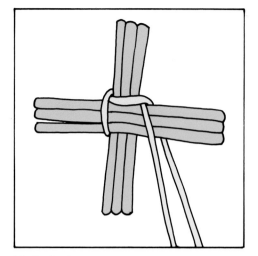

10a Beginning pairing

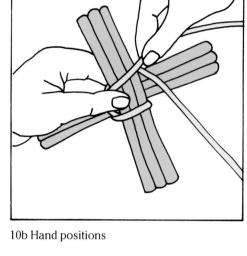

10b Hand positions

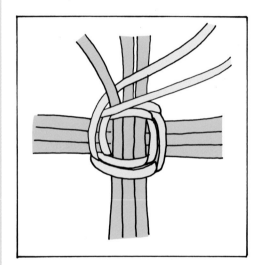

11a Opening out the first stick

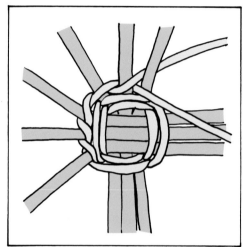

11b Continuing opening out the sticks

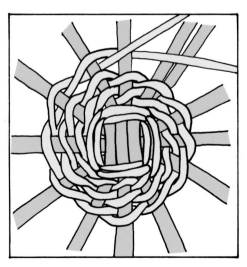

12 Adding an extra stick into the pairing

Completing the Base

1 Begin pairing (Fig 10a,b).

2 Open out the sticks after two or three rows of pairing. Pull the weavers down firmly at the back of the work before bringing round to the front. Hold the weavers securely to keep the work tight and even (Fig 11a,b).

3 It is also possible to add in an extra stick at this stage if required (Fig 12).

4 Continuing the weaving. It is important to aim at all the sticks becoming evenly spaced and to concentrate on avoiding an uneven shape. Bases should be either flat or slightly convex, where extra strength is required. Convex bases can

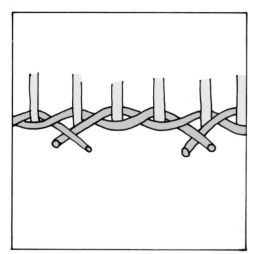

13a Butt-end joins

13b Tip-end joins

be worked either towards or away from the worker.

5 If the weavers are not long enough to reach right round the base and overlap themselves, you will need two or more sets of weavers. Start with tip ends on opposite sides of the base.

Base Weaves

Pairing is the most-used base weave. It is a balanced weave, so helps to control the stakes. French randing is sometimes used after the sticks have been opened out. It is very neat but hard to control. It is possible to start a rand with butts or tips. Slewing is occasionally used on bases, but its primary purpose is speed as it is very hard to keep under control.

Joins must be appropriate to the weaves used, although in baskets for certain purposes, it is possible to make all the joins on one side (Fig 13a,b).

Finishing Off

Finish the base with tip ends and tuck them into the last row of the weaving.

Staking Up

The stakes, which form the structure of the basket sides, must be chosen with care. They must be of equal thickness and strong enough to support the basket. They must also be of suitable thickness at the border height for turning down a border. Two stakes are required for each stick end on the base, minus one if an odd number is required.

1 Slype the butt ends of the stakes. For flaired or straight-sided baskets, slype on the inside of the curve. For bowl shaped baskets, slype on the outside.
2 If using centre cane, cut stakes long enough to insert into the base, plus the height of the basket, plus the length required for the chosen border.
3 Use a bodkin to make a channel into the base as near to the centre as possible, without distorting the base. Stake up with the under side of the base facing upwards.
4 Insert one stake each side of each stick, slype facing upwards, so that the whole structure makes a dish shape.

(*above*) Pricking up with a knife

(*left*) Tied stakes and hooped stakes ready for the upsett

Starting a four-rod wale in two places for the upsett

Pricking Up

1 Turn the base over so that the inside of the basket is now facing upwards.

2 If the willow is well prepared and not too thick, each stake can be kinked at about ¼in (5mm) from the edge of the base, either with the thumbnail or the back of a knife.

3 Tougher material must be pricked up with a knife. Insert the knife just into the surface of the rod, so that the blade is in the same direction as the lie of the rod. Then twist it and lift the rod at the same time.

4 If using centre cane, squeeze it at the same point with round-nosed pliers.

5 Either tie the tip ends together or use a hoop to hold the rods up.

The Upsett

This is the first inch or so of the side of the basket, its purpose being to separate the stakes evenly and set them up at the correct angle, ready to proceed with the basket. The weave used for this is waling.

The first round is done with the base on its side so that a rim is put round it (unless there is to be a foot border). Use a four-rod wale, starting with the butts in two or more places to make a firm edge. After this round, it may be necessary to rap the stakes into the base.

At the end of the first round, change the four-rod wale to three, by dropping one of the weavers (Fig 14). Then continue with the basket the right way up, weighted down or spiked onto a plank. Rap down the weaving after the second round. Continue for an inch or two until the stakes are even and secure, and finish with tip ends. Rap the upsett down to even the height all the way round.

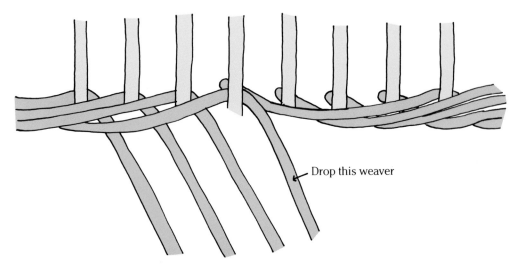

14 Changing from a four-rod wale to a three-rod wale

Bye Stakes

When using centre cane, insert bye stakes after the upsett. If a cane has been chosen of the appropriate size to turn down a border, bye stakes are needed to give the basket enough strength.

Cut these from the same thickness of cane as the stakes, and to the height of the finished basket. (They are not required for the border.) Insert each bye stake to the right of each stake so that the border will cover the ends (Fig 15).

Other types of bye stakes are used in fitching.

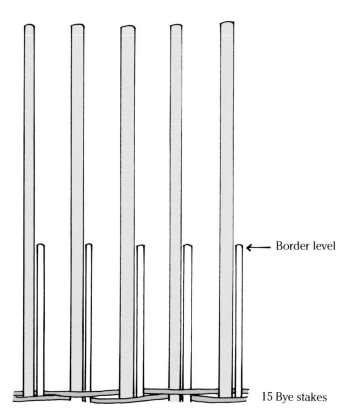

15 Bye stakes

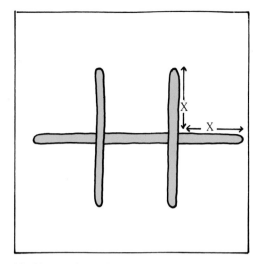

16a Placing the width sticks

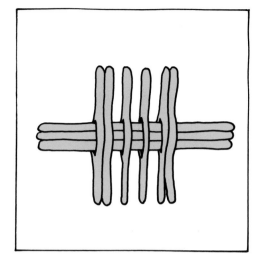

16b Threading the sticks through

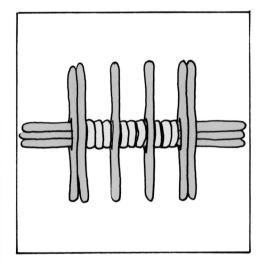

17a Wrapped sticks

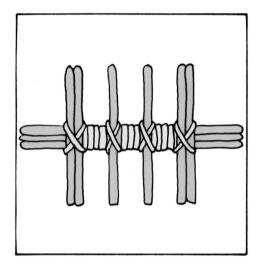

17b Wrapped sticks with crossed wrapping

FRENCH OVAL BASES

There are essentially two methods of constructing an oval base, one which is most commonly seen in French basketry and the other traditional in England.

1 Cut sticks the required length of the oval, plus an inch or so extra. Three sticks will be required for a straight-sided basket, four or five will be necessary for a flowed one.

2 To calculate the number of sticks required for the width, place two sticks across a length stick so that the distance from the end is equal to half the width (Fig 16a).

3 Double sticks are needed at each end, the remainder being evenly spaced across the centre at a suitable distance for weaving (Fig 16b).

4 Pierce the short sticks and thread the long ones through, arranging them as in the diagram.

5 The sticks can also be wrapped with a skein or some chair seating cane for a more decorative effect (Fig 17a,b).

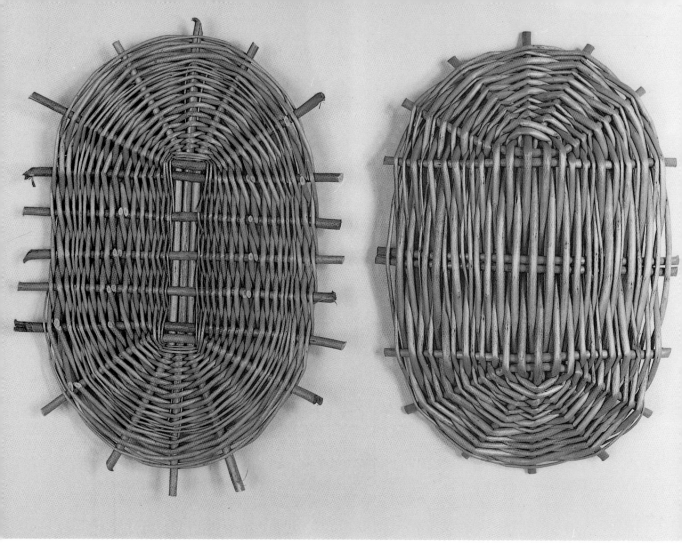

Beginning the Weaving

French base viewed from underneath. English base viewed from the top

Use two sets of weavers on an oval base to avoid one-sidedness or too many joins in one place. Use tips or butts as for round bases, beginning one set at each end of the oval.

Sets of two or four weavers can also be started on the sides rather than the ends (Fig 18a,b).

Continuous use of pairing on an oval tends to distort the shape. Various methods have been devised to counteract this.

a) Pairing on the ends, randing on the sides (Fig 19).
b) Reverse pairing on alternate rows (Fig 20a).
c) Reverse pairing from the halfway point or in blocks (Fig 20b).

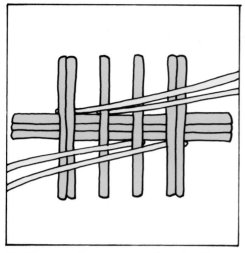

18a Two sets of weavers started on the sides

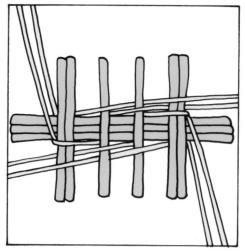

18b Four sets of weavers started on the sides

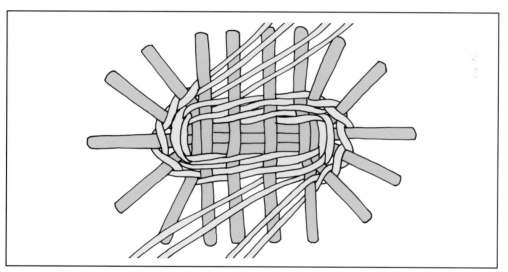

19 Pairing on the ends, randing on the sides

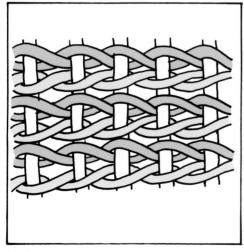

20a Reverse pairing on alternate rows

20b Reverse pairing in blocks

Continuing Weaving

Concentrate on maintaining the shape, not allowing the base to twist. Open out the end sticks after two rounds. Join and shape as for round bases.

Staking Up

Follow the general instructions for staking up round bases, but use double stakes on the ends and single stakes on the sides. Work the upsett as for round bases.

Staked-up French oval base showing detail of double stakes on the ends and singles on the sides

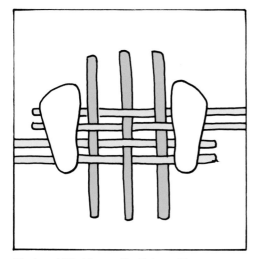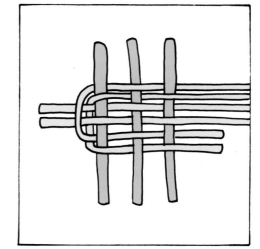

21a,b,c,d Working an English oval base

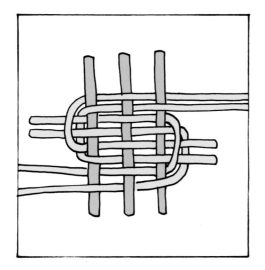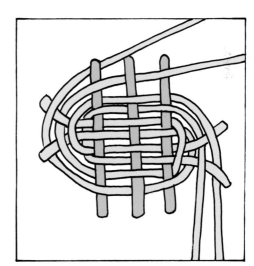

ENGLISH OVAL BASES

There are several variations on this method, but essentially the long sticks of the base are also the weavers, which means they are sturdier than the French type.

The base is worked under foot since more than a pair of hands is required to hold everything in position. It is difficult to do close, neat work at first; it requires a lot of practice.

Making the Base

Example 1 (Figs 21a,b,c,d) uses four long sticks and three cross sticks.

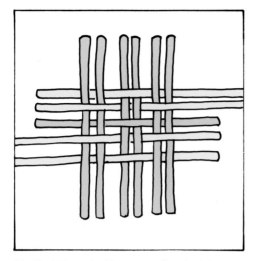

22a English oval with an extra 'long' stick

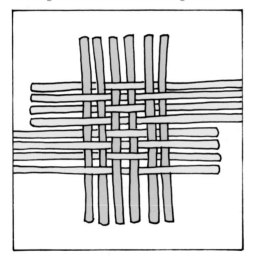

22b English oval with eight long sticks and six cross sticks

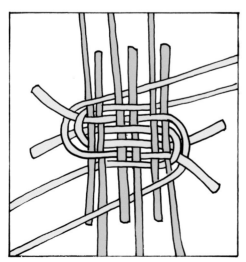

22c English oval cross sticks become side stakes

Example 2 (Fig 22a) is similar to example 1 but incorporates an extra 'long' stick, giving a centre to the end of the base, and uses more cross sticks to make the oval longer.

Example 3 (Fig 22b) uses eight long sticks and six cross sticks to give a much wider base. Weave the inner pairs of weavers first.

Example 4 (Fig 22c) uses uncut rods for the cross sticks so that at the end of the base they become the side stakes.

It is possible to vary this base in many ways, using different numbers of sticks, which can be double or single, giving a slightly different shape to the oval.

Continuing the Weaving

After two rounds of randing, open out the long sticks at the ends. Then continue with randing along the sides and pairing at the ends (Fig 19). Depending on the type of base required, the cross sticks may or may not be opened out in the base weaving.

Staking Up

Follow the general instructions for staking up French oval bases. However, because the cross sticks on an English oval base are more widely spaced, use double stakes on the sides as well as the ends. The upsett is worked the same as for a round base.

SQUARE BASES

All rectangular work is known as square work, as 'square' refers to the angles, not the shape. Sticks are usually cut from the butt ends of stout rods. However where flatness is more important than strength, two or three finer sticks can be used side by side instead. It is easier to keep the base sticks straight if you work with them dry. Alternate butts and tips with double sticks on the outside edges. Using double sticks prevents the outside stick twisting during staking up. Since the right-hand edge of a square base tends to pull in more, make sure that the weaver is positioned so that it always goes behind the right-hand edge stick when weaving from left to right (Fig 23).

Screwblock Method

1 Shave the butt ends of alternate sticks to the same thickness as the tip ends to ensure that the screwblock will hold all the sticks in place (Fig 24).
2 Insert the sticks into the screwblock, evenly spaced to the required width.
3 Begin weaving with a row of pairing by looping enough of the butt end to reach across the base (Fig 25).

continued overleaf

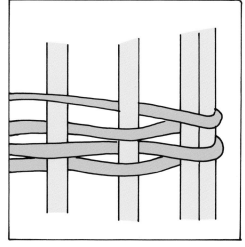

23 Correct way of working round the right-hand edge stick

24 Using a screwblock showing double-edge sticks, shaved to fit

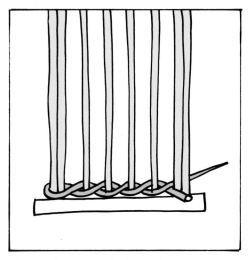

25 Row of pairing at the beginning

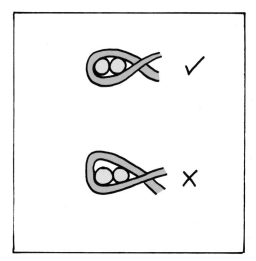

26 Correct way of taking the weaver round the edge sticks

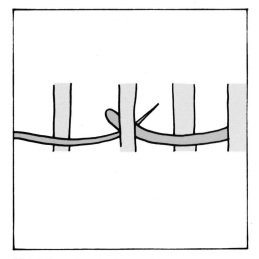

27 Joining with a butt every time

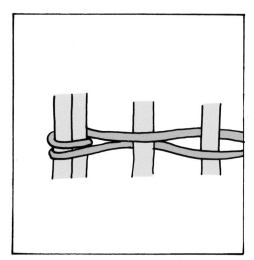

28 Making an extra wrap round the edge sticks

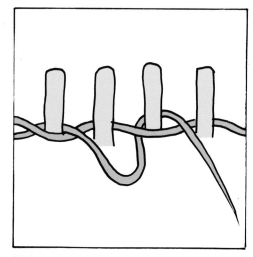

29 Last row tucked under to simulate pairing

4 Continue the weaving by randing with a single rod, paying particular attention to taking the weaver around the side sticks (Fig 26).

5 Join with a butt end every time (Fig 27).

6 Measure frequently to keep the sides parallel.

7 Keep the weaving even by either constant rapping down or making an extra wrap around the double sticks every few rows (Fig 28).

8 Tuck the last woven row under the previous row to simulate pairing (Fig 29).

Seated Method

1 Tie the end pairs of sticks together at top and bottom, and place in position on a bench between nails marking out the correct size (Fig 30).

2 Secure by sitting on top of a tied bunch of willow tips laid across the centre.

3 Begin weaving at the centre with a tip end. Continue randing with a single rod, always joining with the butt end.

4 If the base is particularly long, trim the ends on the back and move the base back underneath you to avoid over reaching.

5 Finish with a pair by using two rods (Fig 31).

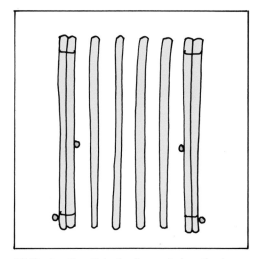

30 Placing the sticks for the seated method

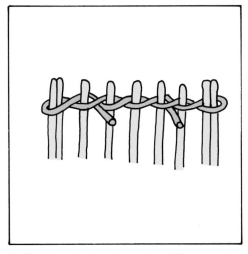

31 Finishing the base by pairing with two rods

6 Turn the base round and work the other end in the same way, then trim all the remaining ends.

Slatted Base

This makes a flatter alternative to a base woven on sticks. Prepare wooden slats by shaving down either side. Use either of the above methods of working a base, bearing in mind that scallomed sides will need single side sticks (Fig 32), whereas an English type of staking up requires double side sticks.

Starting a square base by the seated method

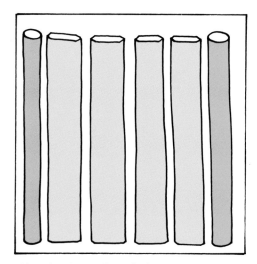

32 Single edge sticks with slats

End stakes interlinked and tied before inserting the side stakes

STAKING UP SQUAREWORK

There are several factors involved in staking up squarework, depending on whether the French or English method is used. Generally the ends are staked up differently from the sides and corners can be worked in various ways.

English Method

Staking Up Sides

Stake up the sides before the ends. Mark the position of the stakes onto the base with a chinagraph pencil which will wipe off easily afterwards. They should be spaced evenly along the sides. If blunt corners are to be used then the end stakes need to be as close to the corner as possible.

1 Cut a straight edge on the belly side of the butt end of the stakes.
2 Insert a well greased bodkin at a slight angle through the side sticks to make a channel for the stakes (Fig 33a). With large work, insert the tip of the bodkin then tap in with a rapping iron. Remove the bodkin and push in the stake with the cut edge facing downwards (Fig 33b).
3 Prick up and tap the stakes in up to the elbow with a rapping iron, then tie them up or use a hoop.

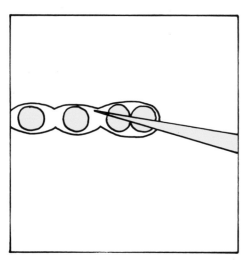

33a Inserting a bodkin into the edge sticks

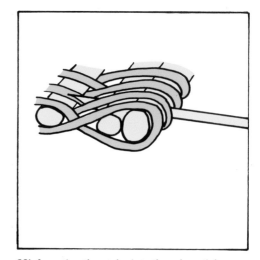

33b Inserting the stake into the edge sticks

Staking Up Ends

Slype the stakes on the belly side and in-sert slype downwards. Ends may require more stakes than the number of sticks on the base (Fig 34). Then prick up the end stakes and tie them or push them into the hoop. They must remain tied at least until the waling is complete.

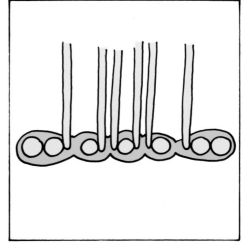

34 Staked-up end showing more stakes than sticks

Corners

a) Blunt corners

This type of corner is not as 'square' look-ing as those with a corner post. Keep the end stakes of the side and end of the basket as close together as possible. When staking up, insert the end stake into the outside edge stick on the base (Fig 35a).

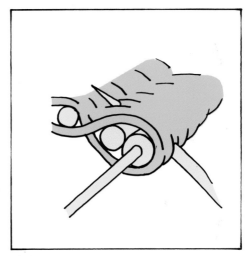

35a Staking up blunt corners

b) English corner posts

Cut the corner posts from stout rods or dowelling to the height of the finished basket plus an inch or so. Shave the in-side edges of the posts for a better fit onto the base and hold in position with a nail. Make a small nick on the outside to help hold the weaving and stop the corner post from slipping (Fig 35b).

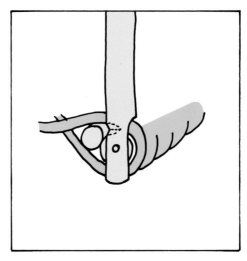

35b Staking up with a corner post

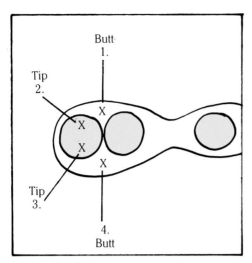

36a Position for inserting weavers for the end wale

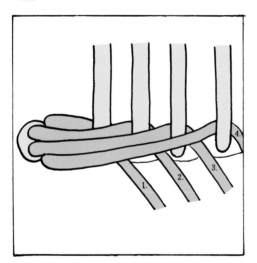

36b Beginning the end wale·

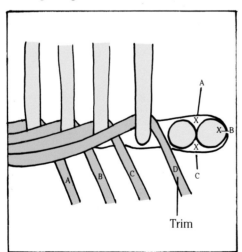

36c Position for cramming off the weavers at the right-hand side

French Method

Staking Up Ends

Stake up the ends as for the English method (see page 62) and tie securely. In order to work the sides in the French method, it will be necessary to work an extra wale across the end stakes as follows.

1 Take four sticks approximately three inches longer than the width of the base.
2 Slype two at the butt end and two at the tip end, and insert into the left-hand end of the base (Fig 36a)
3 Weave each rod once as shown (Fig 36b), and wale to the end.
4 Kink, slype and insert the first three rods and trim off the fourth. Rap into place firmly (Fig 36c).

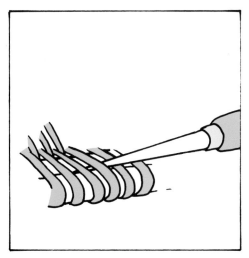

37a Making a channel between the edge sticks

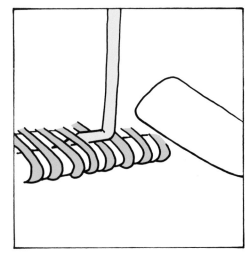

37b Tapping the stake into place

Staking Up Sides

1 Make a straight cut on the back of the rod.

2 With a bodkin, make a channel under the weaving between the double rods on the edge of the base (Fig 37a).

3 Push the end of the rod in with the cut side up, then kink about an inch away from the end, bend upright and tap into place with a rapping iron or bodkin end (Fig 37b).

4 The left-hand stake on each side must be treated differently to prevent the end protruding beyond the edge of the base. Slype the end of a stake, insert it between the two edge sticks and trim off level underneath (Fig 37c).

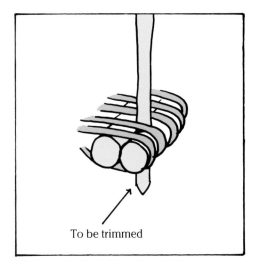

To be trimmed

37c Inserting the left-hand end stake

Corner Posts

Cut the posts, ideally from dowelling, to the height of the finished basket plus an inch or so. Tap a small nail into the bottom end of the corner post to about halfway. Then nip off the head of the nail so that the now sharp end can be tapped into the base (Fig 38).

38 Inserting the corner post

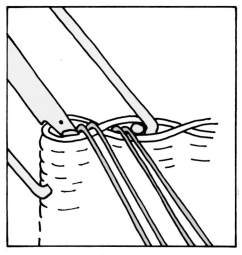

39 Beginning the upsett by the English method

The Upsett

The French Method
This is worked with a three-rod wale, started with tip ends at the left-hand corners. Use two sets of weavers for a small upsett, four sets for a deeper one.

The English Method
Slype the butt ends and insert in pairs into the two spaces closest to the left-hand corner post on the ends (Fig 39).

Corners
During the working of the upsett, keep the stakes as close to the corner posts as possible to keep them tightly in position (Figs 40a,b). The two corner stakes of blunt corners should also be close together. To help with shaping, release them from the ties as soon as possible. Work to prevent the sides from bulging out and the corners becoming rounded.

Joins
Make joins at the centre of the sides or the ends. Finish the upsett with tips at the right-hand corners by choosing weavers of the correct length.

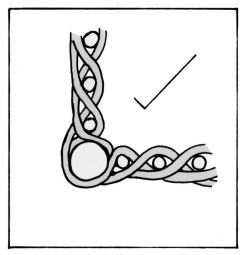

40a Correct way of working to keep the corners square

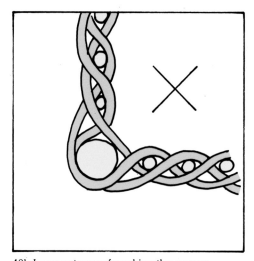

40b Incorrect way of working the corner

SCALLOMED BASES

One of the advantages of scallomed bases is that any shape can be made. The hoop which forms the structure can be shaped round a mould or between strategically placed nails on a board or bench (Fig 41). Soak and mellow the material used thoroughly or use it in its 'green' state, then leave to dry.

'Le cœur à fromage', a traditional French basket

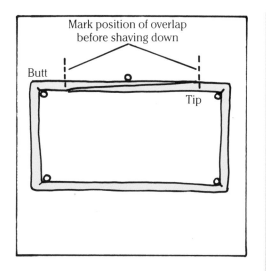

41 Shaping a square hoop

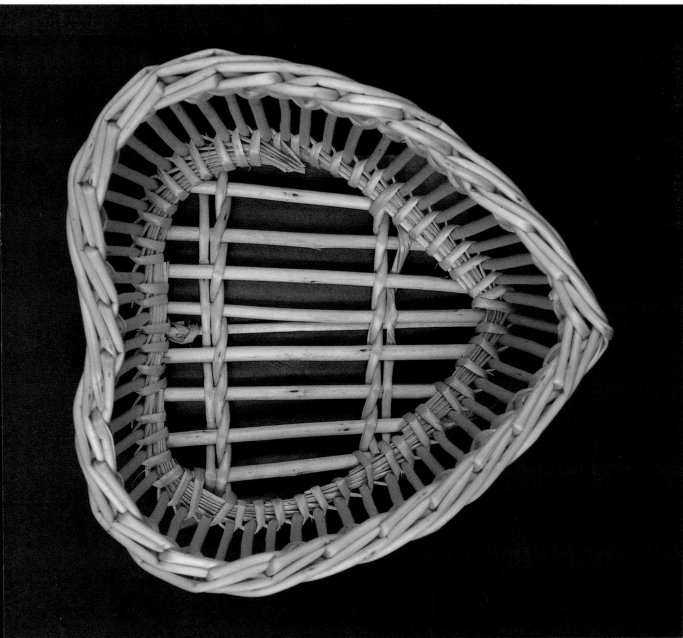

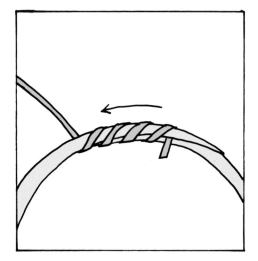

42a Beginning to wrap the overlap

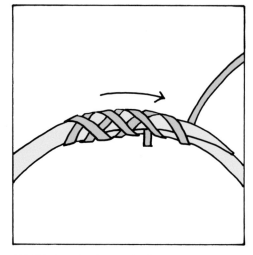

42b Working back over the first wrap

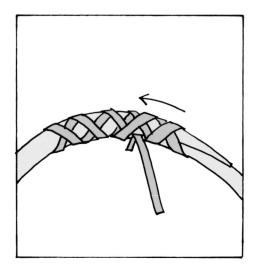

42c Securing the end of the wrapping

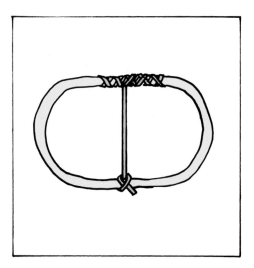

43 Tying an oval to hold the shape

Round Hoop

Make the overlap with the butt on the outside, shaved carefully so that the overlapping ends match. Either glue and temporarily tie or bind it with a skein to hold it in position. Begin with a tip end, weave across the overlap, back over itself, then thread through (Figs 42a,b,c).

Oval Hoop

Bind in the same manner, with the overlap on the long side. Instead of threading the end through, take it across to the other side of the oval and tie to hold the shape (Fig 43).

Square Hoop

Form around nails on the bench (Fig 41), using an extra nail to hold the join, and tie with a skein like an oval (Fig 43).

U-Shaped Hoop

Bend to shape and tie across to hold (Fig 44a).

D-Shaped Hoop

Bend to shape and tie across to hold, kinking both ends at right angles (Fig 44b).

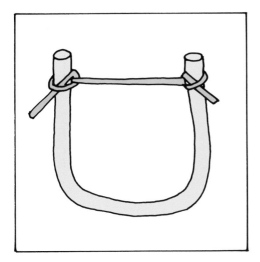

44a Tying a U-shaped hoop

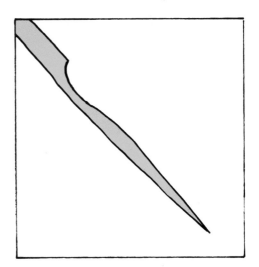

44b Tying a D-shaped hoop

Cutting Scalloms

Cutting scalloms is an acquired skill which takes practice to avoid much wastage. A curved knife is best. Scalloms should be a good few inches long depending on the basket, forming a 'tail' at the butt end of each stake.

1 Cover your lap with a piece of leather or thick fabric to protect clothing from wear.
2 Hold the rod steady with the left hand resting on the knee, palm upwards. Keep the forearm and wrist straight while cutting towards you so that it is impossible to cut yourself.
3 Alternatively, if using a stanley knife or similar, cut away from you.
4 Cut the scallom 'tail' long enough to go round the base, over itself and under the next two stakes (Fig 45a,b,c).

Cutting scalloms

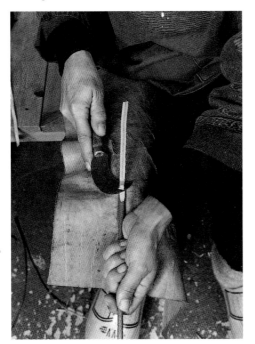

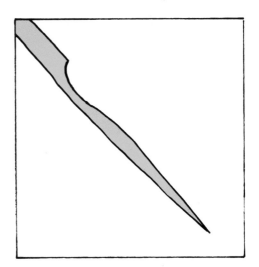

45a Shape of cut scallom

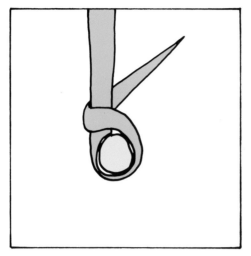

45b Cross section showing how the scallom fits round the hoop

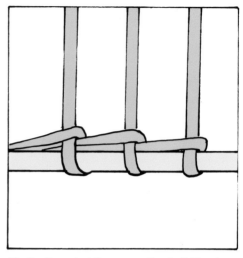

45c Scalloms holding preceding 'tails' in place

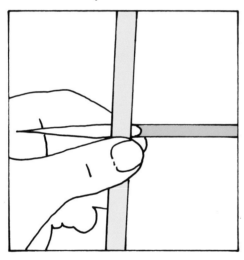

46a Holding the stake in position

46b The stake bent over the hoop

Attaching Scalloms

1 Mark the positions for the scallomed base sticks on the hoop.

2 Sit the hoop on your lap with the join towards you.

3 Place a scallom under the hoop with the tail towards the left (Fig 46a).

4 Bend the stake over the rim (Fig 46b).

5 Fold the tail over itself (Fig 46c).

6 Each succeeding scallom holds the previous two in place.

7 Weave the last scallom tail back round the rim and across at least the previous two to hold it in position.

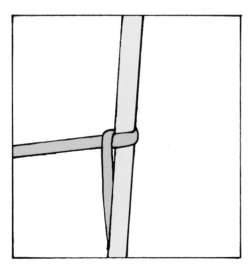

46c Scallom 'tail' folded over the stake

Weaving Round, Oval or Square Scallomed Bases

1 Weave as close to the beginning as possible starting with a tip end (Fig 47a), taking extra turns at the sides as required (Fig 47b). Take care to weave round the back of the right-hand outside edge when working from left to right.

2 Make joins with the butt end each time, either anywhere at the back or evenly along the sides. If the joins are on the sides, the tips will be above and the butts below, or *vice versa* (Fig 47c).

3 After a few rows of weaving, straight cut the tip ends of an equal number of sticks (the tips must be the same thickness as the originals) and thread them down beside the scallomed butts to protrude beyond the base hoop. This gives extra strength without bulk and makes a slightly flatter base.

4 Weave as far as possible up the base before scalloming the other end. The last few rows of weaving will have to be threaded through carefully to avoid kinks.

Weaving U-Shaped Scallomed Bases

1 Scalloms can be attached as for other shaped bases.

2 The tip ends of the sticks can be bordered off or turned up and used as side stakes.

Staking Up with Scalloms

Scallomed stakes are attached in the same way as sticks on the base, but thread the tail of the last one through the first one or two to hold in position. Attach the scalloms with the base between the knees lengthwise. Towards the end it will be necessary to place the base crosswise to avoid damaging the stakes (see photographs overleaf).

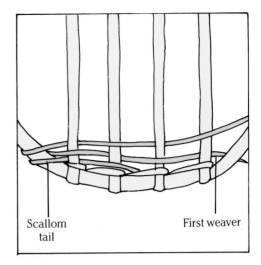

47a Beginning the weaving

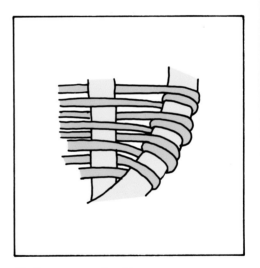

47b Extra turns at the sides

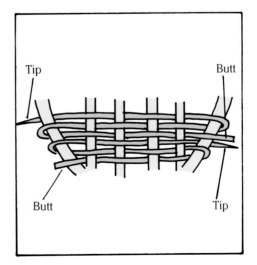

47c Joining at the sides

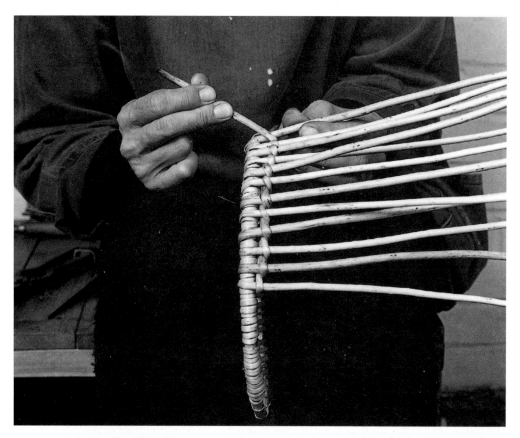

Scalloming onto a Woven Square Base

It is possible to scallom the side stakes onto a woven square base which has not itself been made by the scalloming method. You need only one outside stick each side of the base. Then add a split stick across the ends as follows.

1 Split a stout rod in half lengthways (see page 41).
2 Kink and insert it beside the edge sticks, with the rounded side facing outwards (Fig 48).
3 Start attaching scalloms at a right-hand corner of the long side, working from right to left (see Figs 45, 46).

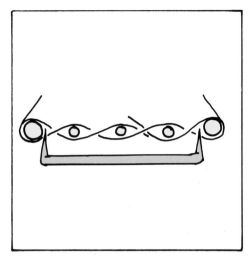

48 Adding a split stick at the end in order to attach scalloms

(Opposite above) Attaching the first scalloms, holding the hoop between the knees;
(Opposite below) Attaching the last scalloms, holding the hoop sideways

(below) Oval basket viewed from below to show slatted fitched base (see overleaf)

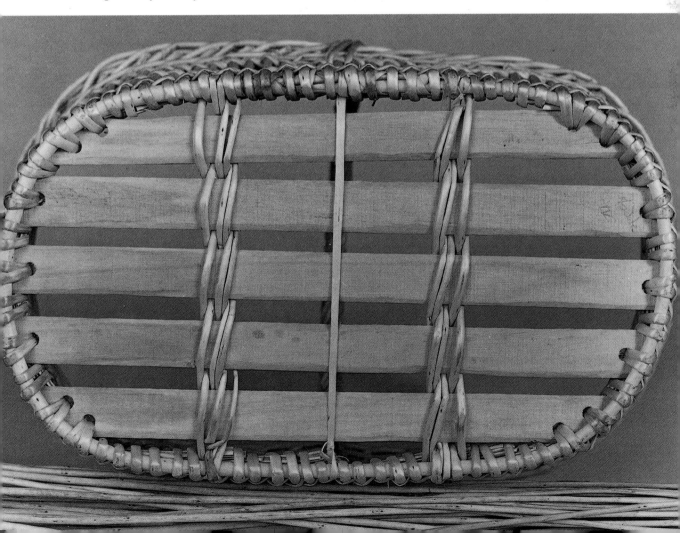

Fitched Bases

Fitching is a weave used to hold the stakes together where openwork is required. There are also particular requirements for using fitching on a base.

1 Make a hoop: round, oval, or square as previously described (See Figs 41-44).
2 Work the base in the seated method.
3 Ensure that the spaces between the base sticks are the same as the thickness of the stakes.
4 Mark the position on the hoop for the fitch.
5 Overlap the tip ends of two weavers so that the tip ends are long enough to reach across the base (Fig 49a).
6 Fitch from left to right across the marked position.
7 At the right side, drop the tips (Fig 49b) and pair backwards across the base to the left (Fig 49c).
8 Measure, tap the two rows of weaving into position with a fitching iron or bodkin, and trim all the ends.

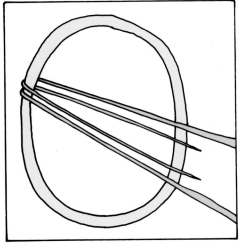

49a Overlapping the tip ends to begin weaving

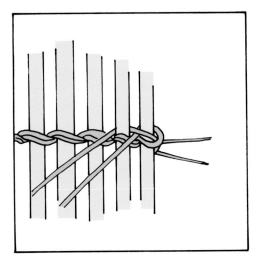

49b Dropping the tips

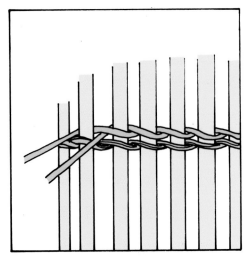

49c Pairing from right to left

Method of dividing the rods for French scallomed stakes

Cutting Scalloms for French Fitched Baskets

In French fitching the stakes are very close together, which means alternate stakes only are needed for bordering down. Because of this and to avoid wastage, cut two stakes from each rod.

1 Choose stakes carefully for suitable thickness and very little taper, making sure the scallom tails are long enough to be tied in by several following stakes (Fig 50). This gives a thick, secure band round the inside of the basket.
2 Cut with the rod under the left arm, working towards you.
3 Shave the scalloms thinly.

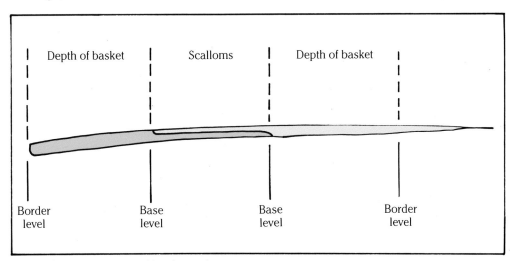

Depth of basket   Scalloms   Depth of basket

Border level   Base level   Base level   Border level

50 Willow rod showing position for cutting scalloms

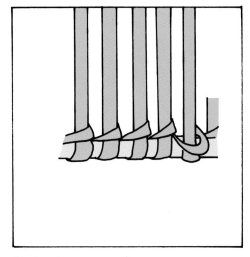

51a Finishing attaching scalloms by threading the end through

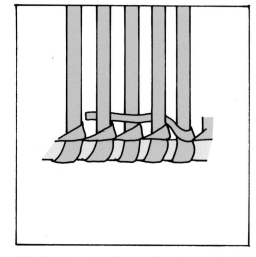

51b Finishing attaching scalloms by weaving the end away

Attaching Scalloms for French Fitching (Round and Oval)

1 Alternate tips and butts, beginning with a top end stake at the centre opposite the join of the hoop.
2 Finish off by either threading through or weaving away (Figs 51a,b).
3 Trim off any spare tails not tied in around the inner rim.

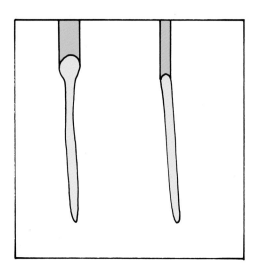

52 Scallomed corner post and scallomed stake

Attaching Scalloms for French Fitching (Square)

1 At the corners, keep at least three scallom tails inside and trim the remainder to make a neat turn.
2 The corner post must be scallomed as well, so scallom the tip end so that the tail is the same thickness and length as the rest (Fig 52).
3 Make sure that the stakes adjacent to the corner posts are both tip end stakes.

Chapter 6
WEAVES

SHAPING

It is very important to concentrate on the shaping of the basket throughout the weaving process. Every stroke involved in any weave should be a positive action to ensure both the stake and the weaver are in the required position.

Stakes should not slope inwards or odd ones lean outwards, neither should they lean to one side or the other. They should never bend around a weaver; weavers do all the bending. Apart from in a few particular techniques, weavers should be finer than stakes.

At least at the end of each complete weave, the work should be measured and rapped down. Close weaving requires rapping down after every row.

Since most weaving is in one direction, there is a tendency to skew the work towards the right. It is simple to counteract this by putting slight pressure in the opposite direction as the work progresses. When making tall square baskets with dowelling corner posts, it is possible to use a rigid cross bar to keep work square. A simple one can be made from plywood with small holes at the corners. Nails tapped into the corner posts can be slipped into the holes (Fig 53).

PAIRING

Pairing is a balanced weave, fairly straightforward to control as it is worked in front of and behind each stake. It is used mainly on round and oval bases.

Weaving

Place two weavers in consecutive spaces. Take the left-hand weaver in front of one stake and behind the next. Repeat this, ensuring that the weavers remain towards you (at the front of the work) after each stroke (Fig 54).

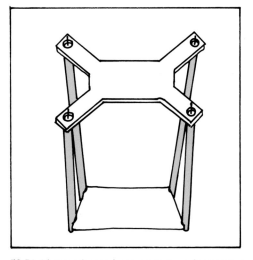

53 Rigid cross bar to keep square work square

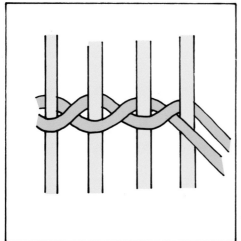

54 Pairing

Joining

Make joins either butt to butt or tip to tip, by one of two methods (Fig 55a,b). It is also possible to make all the joins on the underside of the work (Fig 55c), or push them into the previous rows of weaving alongside a stake (Fig 55d).

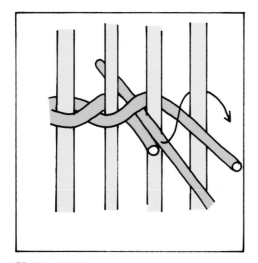

55a Simple join

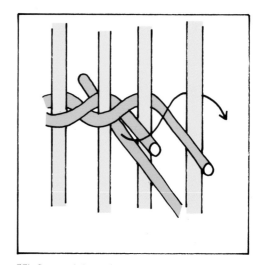

55b Secure join

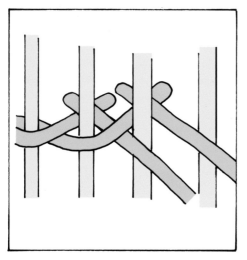

55c Joining on the underside

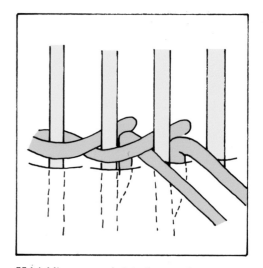

55d Adding new rods into the weaving

Baskets in buff, white, brown and steamed
willow, using a variety of weaves and
techniques

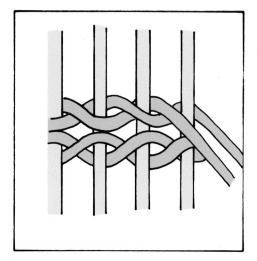

56a Chain pairing

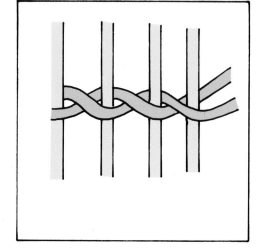

56b Reverse pairing

Chain Pairing

This is a decorative version of the weave, worked on alternate rows. Work the first row normally but the second by taking each weaver underneath the other weaver as it goes round the stake (Fig 56a).

Reverse Pairing

This is identical in appearance to the second row of chain pairing, but it is worked differently. It is used for some of the weaving on an oval base to counteract the twist. Keep the weavers at the back of the work (away from you) after each stroke (Fig 56b).

WALING

Waling is a strong secure weave, used where extra control is required to hold stakes in position, for example at the upsett of a basket or at a point where shaping is wanted. When changing from one weave to another, it is useful to put in a band of waling, partly to delineate the different patterns of weaves, partly for additional strength and partly to keep the stakes under control. It is worked with three or more weavers, repeating the stroke each time with the left-hand rod, however many rods are used. Willow workers will normally begin waling with tip ends of the weavers for a smooth and gradual start. However where a thicker ridge is required, as on the upsett of a basket, the wale is begun with the butt ends.

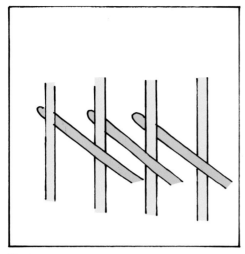

57a Inserting three weavers

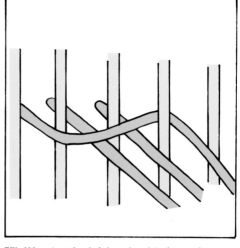

57b Weaving the left-hand rod in front of two, behind one

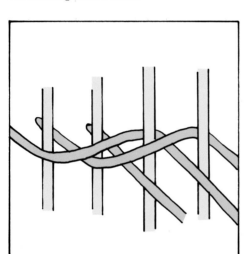

57c Weaving the second rod

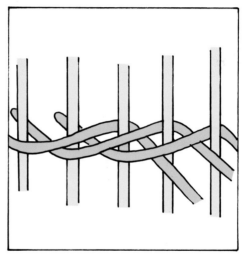

57d Weaving the third rod

Three-Rod Wale

Insert three weavers into three adjacent spaces. Take the left-hand weaver each time in front of two stakes and behind one (Fig 57a,b,c,d).

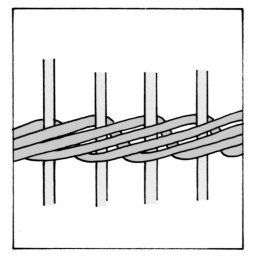

58a Four-rod wale in front of three, behind one

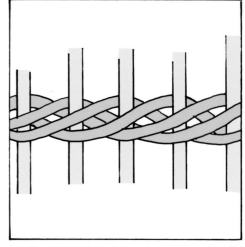

58b Four-rod wale in front of two, behind two

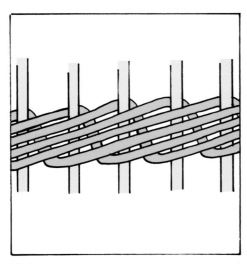

59 Five-rod wale

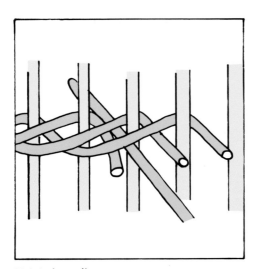

60 Join for waling

Four-Rod Wale

The four-rod wale can be worked in two ways. First insert four weavers into four adjacent spaces then, depending on the purpose of the weave choose either of the following methods.

a) Take the left-hand weaver in front of three stakes and behind one, repeat the stroke each time (Fig 58a).
b) Where both sides of the weave are required to look the same, take the left-hand weaver in front of two stakes and behind two (Fig 58b).

Five-Rod Wale (Fig 59)

Five or more rods can be used in a wale on the same principle, larger wales being used to make a ridge around the basket, either for decorative purposes or to act as a ledge for a lid (see trunk wale).

Joins

Join either tip to tip or butt to butt by pushing the new end into the weaving alongside the old one (Fig 60). When working with cane, the joins will be less frequent and preferably not at the same place each time.

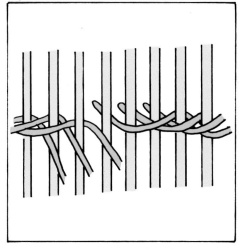

61a The end of the first round ready to step up

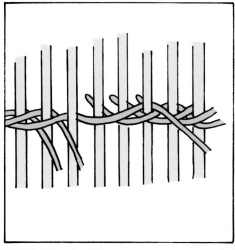

61b Working the right-hand weaver

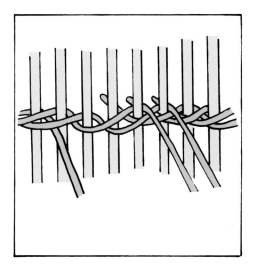

61c Working the centre weaver

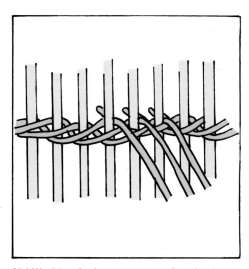

61d Working the last weaver, ready to begin the second round

The Step Up (for a three-rod wale)

The fine tip end of a willow rod allows for a level finish to a band of waling. Since centre cane is of even thickness, the band of waling becomes a very evident spiral. To make each round complete in itself it is necessary to work a step up (Fig 61a,b,c,d).

1 Work the wale until the right-hand weaver is in the space before the first weaver at the beginning of the round.

2 Take the right-hand weaver in front of two and behind one stake.

3 Repeat the stroke with the middle weaver.

4 Repeat the stroke with the left-hand weaver.

5 Begin the next round with the left-hand weaver (the one which has just been worked).

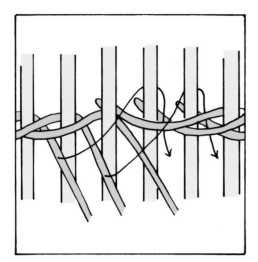

62 Completing a round

Finishing

To finish a band of waling in willow, just taper away to nothing with the tip ends.

To finish a band of waling in cane, the ends need to be threaded under the weavers at the beginning to complete the weave (Fig 62).

Chain Wale

This variation on the basic weave can be used for decorative effect. Work the first row as normal. On the second round, take the left-hand weaver under (not over) the other weavers as you work round the stake (Fig 63a,b).

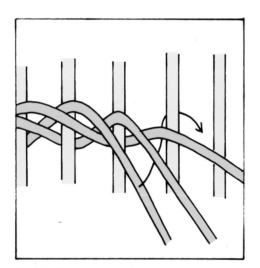

63a Working a chain wale

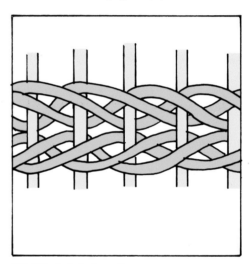

63b Effect of chain waling

Square Corners

On square baskets which have corner posts the sharp corner can be accentuated by changing the stroke of the weave (Fig 64).

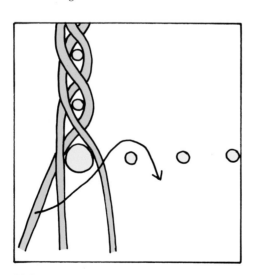

64 Changing the stroke round a square corner

Large white willow hamper with fitched drop-in tray showing the trunk wale (*Ben Braster*)

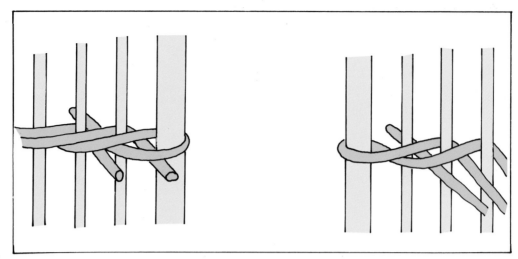

65 Waling from edge to edge

Waling Round a Notch

Where a space is required in the basket, for example the front of a dog basket, begin the waling to the right of the notch and finish on the left so that each row is complete in itself (Fig 65).

The Trunk Wale

This is a very thick row of five-rod waling near the top of a basket to act as a ledge on the outside for a lid to rest on. It is usually followed by a trac border, sloped towards the inside of the basket, for the lid to fit over.

1 Choose rods carefully so that the wale will be fairly even all the way round the basket. At least two sets will be required. Measure the length for each set of weavers from the centre front of the basket to the centre back and trim off excess tip ends.
2 Start the wale with tip ends at the centre back of the basket, being careful to control the weave as the weavers are considerably stronger than the stakes. Join in the second set of weavers with their butt ends at the centre front. On very large baskets, where the wale needs to be particularly wide, kink the weavers at the appropriate distance out from the basket as you work the weave.
3 At the end of the round thread the ends into the weave at the beginning to make the wale continuous (see Fig 62).

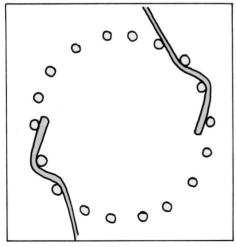

66a Beginning slewing in two places if there is an even number of stakes

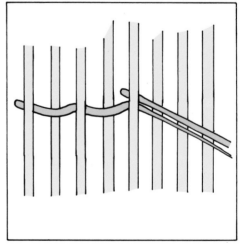

66b Adding in the second rod

SLEWING

Slewing is a useful weave for speed and for using up oddments of willow. However it is difficult to control, especially when using a large number of weavers. If it is used in conjunction with other weaves, it is best done at the beginning of the basket where the stakes are thicker and therefore the slew is easier to control.

Two-Rod Slew

This is the simplest and easiest to control.
1 Start with the butt ends. If there is an even number of stakes, start the weave in two places on opposite sides of the basket alongside an alternate stake (Fig 66a).
2 Work in front of one stake and behind the next until half way along the length of the rod. Add in a second rod above the first and work them together (Fig 66b).
3 When the first rod reaches its tip end, leave the tip on the outside, add in a third rod above the second and continue weaving with these two (Fig 66c).
4 Continue weaving in this manner, adding in one more rod on top as the lower one is used up.
5 To finish, just weave the last tip to its end.

Three-, Four-, Five- and Six-Rod Slew

It is possible to work a slew with a much larger number of rods, bearing in mind that the more rods there are the harder it is to control. It is essential that the stakes remain upright and that all the bending is done by the weavers.
1 Begin by adding in the required number of weavers at regular intervals along the length of the first weaver as you weave it (Fig 67a).
2 Work on the same principle as a two-rod slew. When the bottom weaver ends, add in another on the top (Fig 67b). However, a more even weave is achieved by adding in the weavers at regular intervals by counting the number of stakes woven rather than at the exact point when the lowest weaver ends.

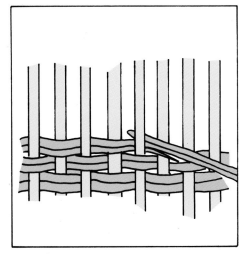

66c Adding in new rods

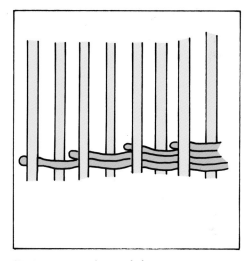

67a Beginning a four-rod slew

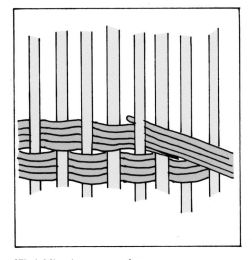

67b Adding in a new rod

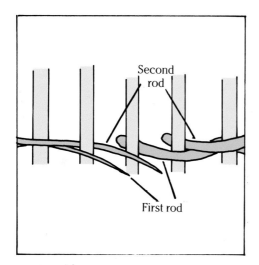

68a Beginning English randing

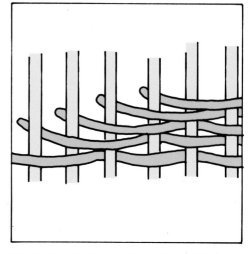

68b Starting English randing in front of two

RANDING

This general term applies to any weave using a single rod woven in front of one stake and behind one. This is the most straightforward weave for cane workers: use a continuous single length and join at the back of the work when the cane is used up. If an even number of stakes are used, two weavers are required, to be placed alternatively. There are several variations of randing which are used to take account of the length and taper of a willow rod.

English Randing

1 Select the same number of weavers as stakes, finer but of similar thickness, preferably long enough to reach right round the basket.
2 Begin with one butt end placed inside the basket, alongside a stake.
3 Work in front of one stake and behind one round the basket until you reach the tip end, but do not overlap the butt of the same rod.
4 Start the second weaver one space to the right of the butt end of the first weaver. It will finish one space to the right of the first tip end (Fig 68a).

As you continue to build up the weaving, one side of the basket will be higher than the other. This will balance out when a complete set of weavers has been randed. A complete rand produces a spiral effect at the point where the tip and butt ends meet. This can be exaggerated by starting the weave in front of two stakes (Fig 68b). The height of the rand will be limited by the thickness of the weavers. If you require a greater height work a second complete rand. (See also Packing with English Randing.)

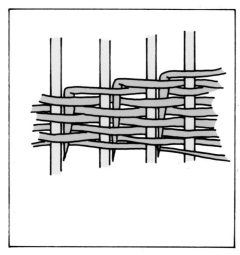

69 Prick randing

Prick Randing

Detail of English randing

Work this the same as English randing, but begin by inserting the slyped butt ends into the weaving (Fig 69).

This is very useful when you do not want any ends inside the basket.

Randing with Flat Material

Baskets can be woven with flat band cane, chair seating cane or willow skeins. This is done in one of two ways.

a) Work the weavers on their edges, overlapping the ends on each complete round (Fig 70a). This is fairly quick to do but not always easy to keep under con-trol, as the weavers are so flimsy.

b) Alternatively, lay the weavers on top of one another, making a half twist between each stake (Fig 70b). This is very slow to do but makes a very closely woven basket.

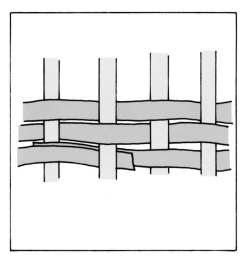

70a Randing with flat material on its edge

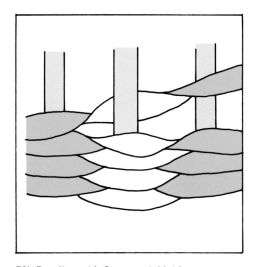

70b Randing with flat material laid on top

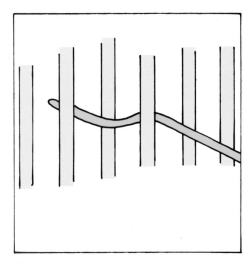

71a Beginning French randing

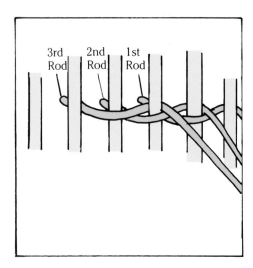

71b French randing with three weavers worked

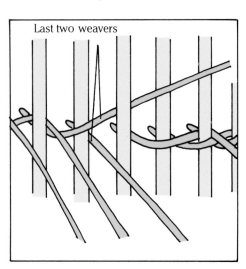

71c Completing the round of French randing

French Randing

1 Choose the same number of weavers as stakes, of similar thickness and length, finer than the stakes.

2 Place the butt end of the first weaver behind a stake. Weave in front of one stake and behind one (Fig 71a). It is possible to work the weave beginning with tips, but it is much more difficult to control.

3 Start the second and subsequent weavers one space to the left of the one just worked, weaving each one in front of one stake and behind one (Fig 71b).

4 At the end of the round it is awkward to fit in the last two weavers. Reach underneath the first two to put them in (Fig 71c). Ensure that there is a weaver in every space around the basket.

5 Work each row of weaving by taking the next weaver on the left in turn, in front of one stake and behind one. At the end of each round you will need to reach under the first two woven in order to weave the last two.

6 Work each round in the same way until the tips are reached. Leave the tips on the inside of the basket, to be trimmed off later. If the next weave in the construction of the basket is to be a wale, the tips can be left on the outside as the ends will be hidden by the greater bulk of the waling.

Log basket in white and buff willow (*Ben Braster*)

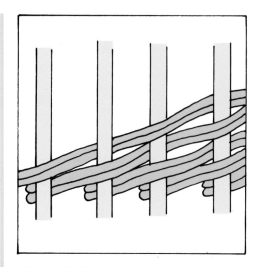

72a Double French randing

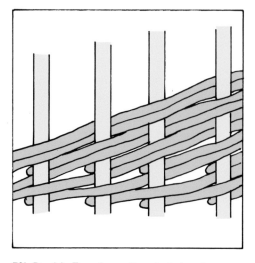

72b Double French randing started on two rows

Double French Randing

Work this in the same way as French randing, using double weavers. This version of the weave will give twice the height of a single rand. It is much neater to begin the second set of weavers on the second round to avoid wedge-shaped gaps at the beginning (Fig 72a,b). As the two weavers together are much stronger, it can be difficult to keep control. Make sure that the pairs of weavers lie one directly above the other and do not cross over each other.

Detail of double French randing

Extra Weavers

In order to achieve a required height without double French randing, either use longer rods or put in extra weavers. Only join in pairs of weavers, otherwise the weave will not work out correctly (Fig 73). You can also add in pairs of weavers all the way round the basket in the same way, giving double the height of the rand while the weave appears the same. To finish a rand containing extra weavers, leave the tips in the same position as the butts at the beginning.

Mock Waling

Working a French rand in front of two and behind one stake creates an effect like waling. It is useful to create a decorative ridge round the basket as part of a normal rand.

Variations

It is interesting to experiment with more than one colour. It is possible to create vertical stripes and spirals quite easily.

Block Weave

This decorative weave is normally close woven so that there are no gaps to be seen anywhere. To achieve this, the

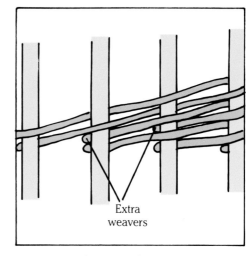

73 Adding in extra weavers for extra height

weave is strongly rapped down after each row.

1 Choose carefully half as many weavers as stakes.
2 Work one weaver in front of two and behind two stakes.
3 Add in the next and subsequent weavers two spaces to the left of the last, and weave in the same way.
4 Work each succeeding rand in the same way, placing the weavers in the alternate spaces (Fig 74).

74 Block weave

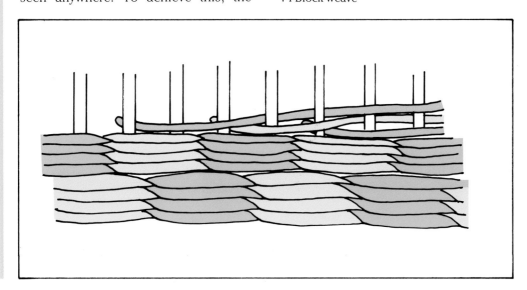

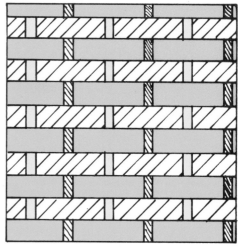

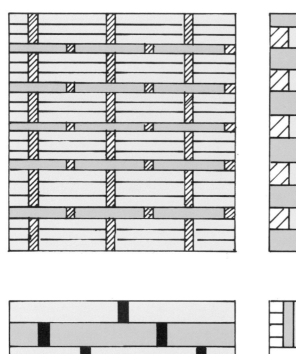

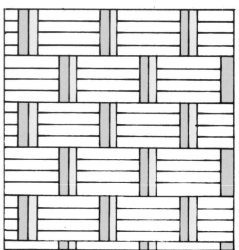

75 Variations on randing

Variations on Weaves

When working with centre cane, more interest can be created by varying and mixing some of the weaves, or using different thicknesses and colours (Fig 75).

Fishing creel showing use of packing

PACKING

Packing is used to build up height on one area of a basket (Fig 76). Several layers of packing can be used, waling if necessary between layers.

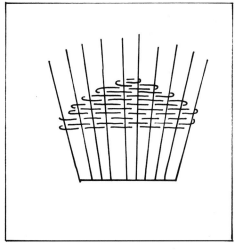

76 Using packing to build up height

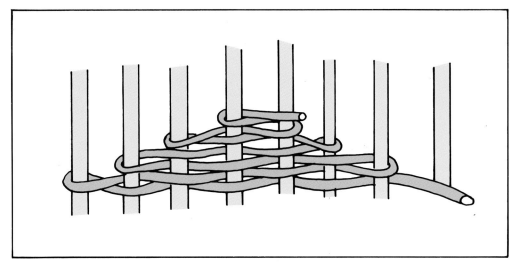

77a Beginning packing at the sides

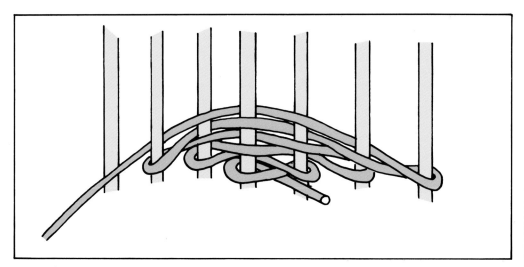

77b Beginning packing at the centre

Working from the Sides
(Fig 77a)

1 Start with a butt end at one side of the area requiring building up.
2 Weaving in front of one stake and behind one work across to the other side.
3 Weave around the end stake and work back towards the beginning.
4 This time stop and work back around the last but one stake.
5 Continue in this way, working round one stake fewer at each side until you reach the centre.
6 Join with a butt end each time (see Fig 27).

Working from the Centre
(Fig 77b)

If more than one layer of packing is required, it is better to start in the centre, increasing the number of stakes woven, then decrease so that all the loops occur at the top and bottom of the work rather than in the middle of the weaving. This method is also used when working inside a curve (Fig 78).

1 Start with the butt end in the space between two stakes at the centre of the area for packing.

2 Work once in a figure of eight around these two central stakes.

3 Continue weaving from side to side, adding in one stake at each side every row.

4 Join with a butt end each time (see Fig 27).

Packing with English Randing

This is an effective method for a square display basket.

1 Choose weavers to reach from front to back and across the back. The number required will be the same as the number of stakes on the two sides of the basket.

2 Starting with the butt end at the right-hand front corner, work from front to back and across the back.

3 Each succeeding rod begins one space to the right.

4 Work half the weavers in this way, so that the last rod will start at the right-hand corner at the back and finish at the left-hand corner at the front (Fig 79a).

5 Turn the basket round and work the remaining half of the weavers in a similar manner on the other side, this time working the weave from right to left (Fig 79b).

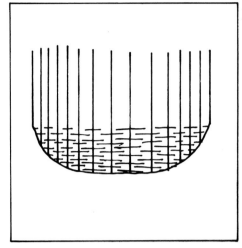

78 Packing inside a curve

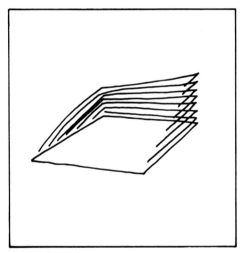

79a First set of weavers for packing with English randing

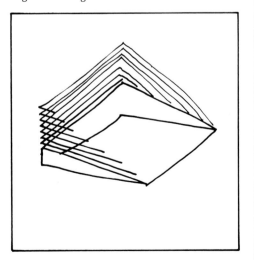

79b Second set of weavers for packing with English randing

FITCHING

Fitching is a weave used after a space. It holds the stakes very firmly in position. Although the effect is very similar to reverse pairing, the method is quite different.

Stakes

Stakes for fitching need to be closer together than for any other weave. Either add in bye stakes after the upsett (Fig 80) or use scalloming to attach the stakes. Scallomed stakes for French fitching must be the thickness of the stakes apart.

Preparation

1 Ensure that the top row of waling on the upsett is securely tucked in, as there will be no weaving above to hold it in place.
2 Mark the position for the rows of fitching on the stakes.
3 Choose two long slender weavers and overlap the tip ends (Fig 81).

Method

1 Loop the overlapping tips of the weavers around a stake.
2 Take the left-hand weaver in the left hand and the right-hand weaver in the right hand, palms downwards. With the right thumb, push the stake into position.
3 Then take the left fist under the right fist and change hands so that the weavers cross.
4 Take the weaver at the back around the next stake each time.
5 Finish the round by joining strategically so that the overlap at the end occurs with tip ends. Reverse pair round the first few stakes until the tip ends taper away to nothing.
6 If a second row of fitching is required higher up the basket, continue fitching at an angle up to the level of the next row. This can look untidy on tall square baskets because the angle occurs on a different side each row. In this case it may be preferable to work each round complete in itself.

Hand positions during fitching

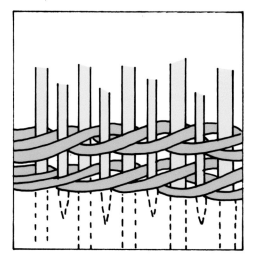

80 Adding bye stakes for fitching

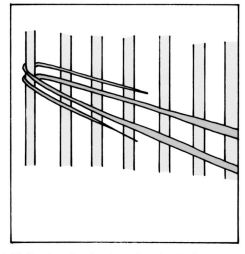

81 Overlapping the tip ends to begin fitching

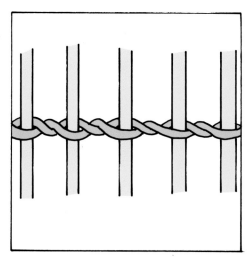

82 Twisted fitch

Twisted Fitch

An extra twist can be put in when the stakes are more widely spaced, to ensure that they are held firmly in position. Also if the basket is to flow out slightly, the extra twist can be used to spread out the stakes (Fig 82).

Joins

1 Tips. When the weavers become too thin, join in new tip ends by working them together for a few strokes (Fig 83a). 2 Butts. Make joins butt to butt ensuring that the joins are a few stakes apart; otherwise the work will be too bulky (Fig 83b).

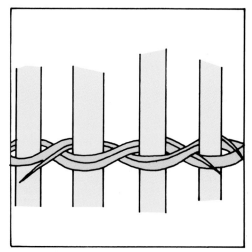

83a Joining fitching with tips

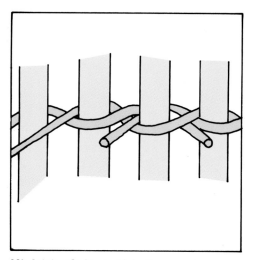

83b Joining fitching with butts

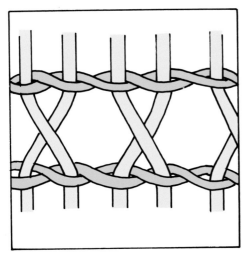

84 Cross fitching

Cross Fitching

Cross the stakes between each row of fitching to create decorative openwork effects (Fig 84).

Finishing Off

1 Cut off the bye stakes about ¼in (5mm) above the fitch.
2 Work a four rod wale behind two (starting with tips), to hide the top of the bye stakes on the first round. Start and finish with tips.
3 Turn the basket upside down and rap down the fitching to close any gap between the fitch and the wale.

Cane Fitching

This method can also be used for fine willow work.

1 Loop the cane around a stake.
2 Hold both the ends in the right hand, palm uppermost. Keeping a firm hold, turn your hand over anticlockwise.
3 Slip the weaver at the back (formerly at the front) around the next stake.
4 Repeat all round the basket, then thread the ends through the loop at the beginning to hold in position.

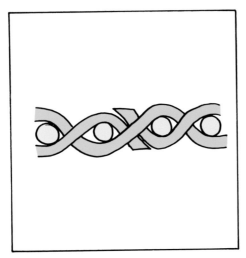

85a Trimmed ends resting on a weaver

85b Trimmed ends resting on a stake

(*above*) Oval shopping basket showing the first row of fitching sloping up to the second row

TRIMMING ENDS

Trimming is either done during the making of a basket or left until it is complete. A picking knife is the traditional method, but it is difficult to do without cutting into the weaving. Most modern basketmakers use a sharp pair of shears or secateurs. Cut the ends close enough so that you cannot feel them when running your hand over the surface of the weaving. Be sure they are securely resting on either a weaver or a stake (Fig 85a,b).

Chapter 7
BORDERS

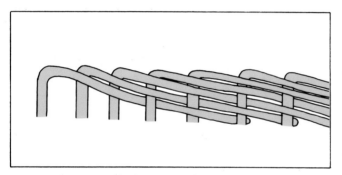

86 Leaving a space at the beginning of a trac border

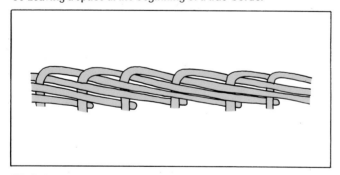

87a Behind-one, in-front-of-two trac

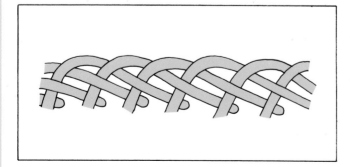

87b Behind-one, in-front-of-one trac

TRAC BORDERS

The trac border is one of the simplest in concept, although it is not always the simplest to execute. It is used where the edge does not need to be strong or bulky and it can be very decorative. It is often used as an edging for flat mats or as a ledge or rim to accommodate a lid.

1 If multiple rods are required, add in extra ones alongside the stakes either on one or both sides.
2 Space must be allowed at the beginning for the rods to thread through at the end to complete the weave (Fig 86).
3 If a sharp edge rather than a smooth curve is required, kink all the rods at the appropriate distance from the edge.
4 The trac is worked in front of and behind the succeeding rods in a regular repeating pattern. Various combinations can be used for different effects (Fig 87a,b,c).

5 Finishing is straight-forward. Just continue the weave in the same way, threading into the spaces left at the beginning. Make sure that each rod lies on top of its predecessor. It is sometimes difficult to do without kinking the rods, so take your time and ease the rods gently through.

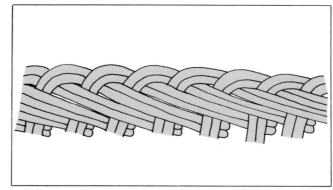

87c Behind-one, in-front-of-two trac, using double rods

Trac Border used as the Sides of a Basket

One method of working this is as follows.

1 Stake up three stakes each side of every base stick and prick or kink them up.

2 Work a trac with the three stakes together, in front of one, behind one, in front of one, behind one and leave the ends to the front (Fig 88).

88 Trac worked with three rods for side of basket

3 Turn the basket upside down. Weave the ends of the stakes into a foot border by working a simple behind-one trac (Fig 89a).

4 Thread the ends through to the underneath of the base by taking each set of ends in turn under the set to the right of them and through to the inside (Fig 89b).

5 Trim all the ends, being careful not to cut them too short.

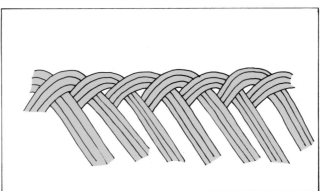

89a Behind-one trac at foot

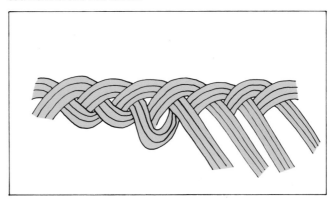

89b Finishing off

Madeira basket with trac border used as sides (*Institute of Agricultural History and Museum of English Rural Life, University of Reading*)

ROD BORDERS

Rod borders are probably most often seen on willow baskets. They can vary from a three-rod, which is no wider than the waling on which it usually sits, up to a six- or seven-rod, giving a lovely thick rolled edge when done properly. It is a very strong border, fairly straightforward in method and relatively easy to avoid spoiling with kinks in the wrong places. The basic principle behind a rod border remains the same whichever border it is.

Three-Rod-Behind-One-Border

1 Bend down three rods in turn each behind its neighbour, and to the front again from left to right. Ensure that the rods are kinked just enough above the top of the weaving to allow space for a rod to thread underneath (Fig 90a).

2 Take the left-hand of these rods in front of one upright stake and behind one, then bend the first upright down alongside it. Do not allow it to rest on top; it must lie alongside (Fig 90b).

3 Repeat the above stroke with rods two and three. There are now three pairs of rods bent down towards you (Fig 90c).

4 The action is the same from now on, taking the right-hand rod of the left-hand pair (in front of one upright and behind one

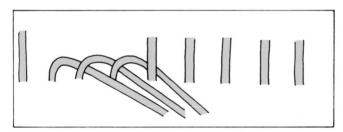

90a Bending down rods for a three-rod border

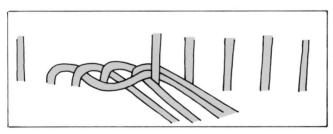

90b Weaving the first rod and bending down the next upright stake

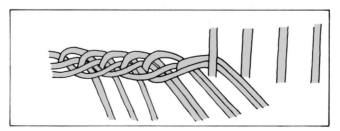

90c Continuing the border

then bend the first upright down alongside it).

5 The last weavers thread under the first loop at the beginning (Fig 91a).

6 Of the remaining three pairs, take the right-hand of each in turn, in front of two stakes and behind one (Fig 91b).

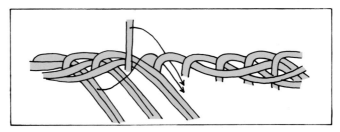

91a Bending down the last upright stake

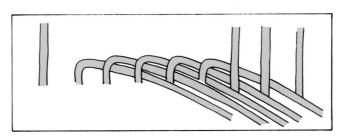

91b Completing the three-rod border

Five-Rod-Behind-Two-Border

1 Bend down five rods, each behind two stakes (Fig 92a).

2 Take the left-hand rod in front of two uprights and behind one. Bend down the first upright alongside it (Fig 92b). Repeat five times so that there are five pairs towards you.

3 Take the right-hand rod of the left-hand pair in front of two uprights and behind one, then bend the first upright down alongside it. Repeat until you reach the beginning.

4 The last two uprights and their corresponding weavers need to be threaded through the first two bent-down stakes.

5 To complete, each right-hand rod of the remaining five pairs is worked in front of four stakes and behind one (Fig 93).

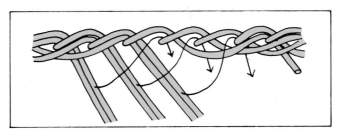

92a Bending down rods for a five-rod border behind two

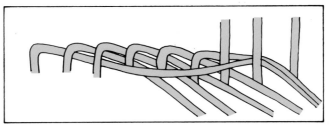

92b Beginning the five-rod border

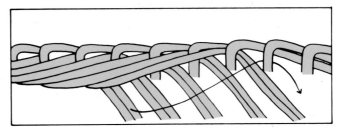

93 Completing the five-rod border

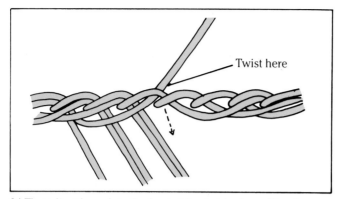

94 Threading through to the front at the finish of a rod border

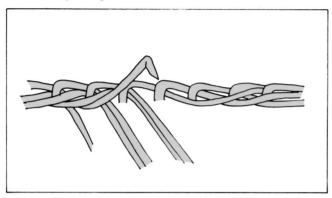

95 Cramming off

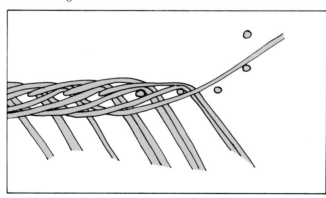

96a Approaching a blunt corner   four-rod-behind two

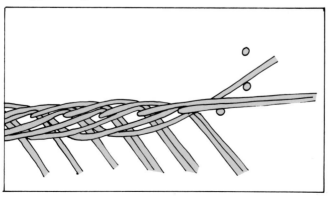

96b Bending down the last two uprights

Finishing Rod Borders

Threading through the last rods to complete the border is often difficult to do without kinks, especially on squarework. It is more easily done by threading the rod to the inside of the basket, giving it a few twists at the back close to the border and then threading it through to the front (Fig 94). (A less than perfect border finish can sometimes be hidden by a handle!)

On lidded squarework, ensure that the border is finished on the hinge side so that any unevenness will be covered by the lid.

On very large baskets or when the willows used are in poor condition, do not thread the rods through, but slype, kink and rap them down alongside the appropriate stake. This is known as cramming off (Fig 95).

Rod Border Structures

The weaving of each stake in a rod border is exactly the same all round the border, including the joining up at the end. If you are uncertain how to proceed at the end, follow the progress of any stake in a completed part of the border. Some of the rod border structures are listed below.

a) *Three-rod-behind-one*
Each stake works behind one, in front of two and behind one.

b) *Four-rod-behind-one*
Each stake works behind

one, in front of three and behind one.

c) *Four-rod-behind-two*
Each stake works behind two, in front of three and behind one.

d) *Five-rod-behind-two*
Each stake works behind two, in front of four and behind one.

e) *Five-rod-behind-two,* alternative version
This version is easier to thread through at the finish. Each stake works behind two, in front of three and behind two.

Square Corners

When doing rod borders with squarework, there are various methods of working the corners in order to make them neat, tight and square. It involves a change of stroke around the corner, the rest of the border being the same. Any rod border can be worked in a similar way round a corner. Some examples are given below.

a) Four - rod - behind - two -border around a blunt corner (Figs 96-8).

b) Four - rod - behind - two -border with a corner post, covering the post. Cut the corner post level with the waling. Slype an extra stake and insert it into the middle of the post or between the post and the outside weaving before working round the corner (Figs 99,100 – overleaf).

c) Five - rod - behind - two - border with a corner post, exposing the post (Figs 101-2 – overleaf).

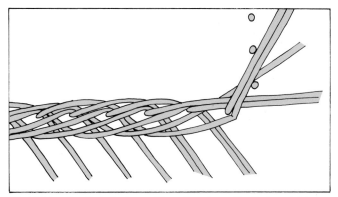

97a Making the first stroke and bending down the first upright

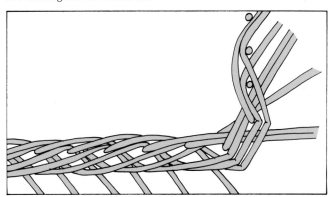

97b Making the second stroke

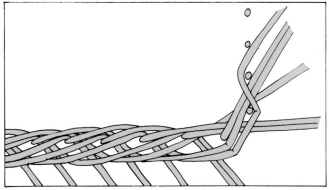

98a The third stroke and bending down the second corner upright

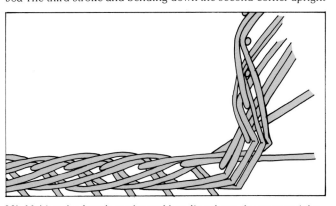

98b Making the fourth stroke and bending down the next upright

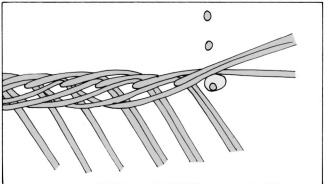

99a First stage showing extra stake inserted into corner post

Four-rod-behind-two border with a corner post, covering the post

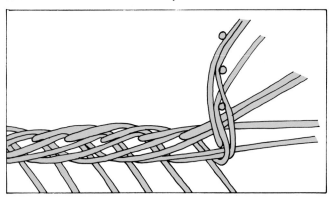

99b First stroke around the corner post

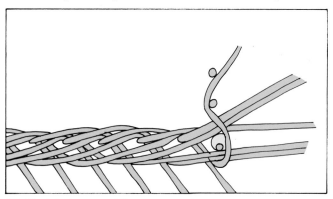

100a Second stroke and extra stake bent down

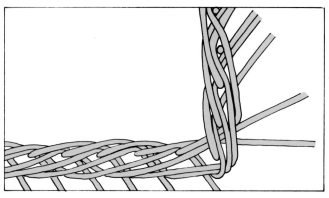

100b Continuing round the border

Five-rod-behind-two border
with a corner post, exposing the post

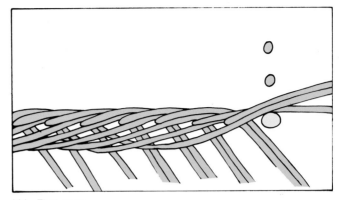

101a First stage

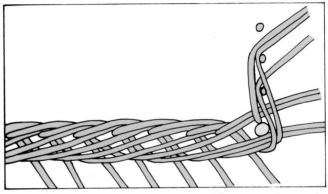

101b Stakes laid alongside corner post and first two strokes made

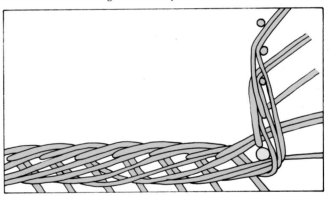

102a Continuation of corner

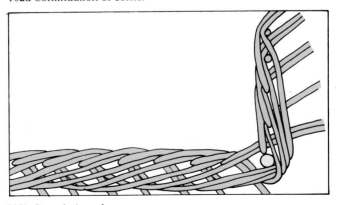

102b Completion of corner

Four-rod-behind-two border showing detail of a blunt corner

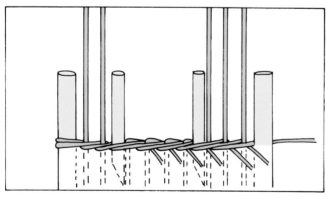

103 Rod border incorporated into a wale on the front end of a square tray

Rod Border across a Notch

Where a notch is required in the basket, it is possible to turn down a rod border to form the gap and incorporate it into a wale at the same level (Fig 103).

1 Add in two posts for the edges of the notch.
2 Work a three-rod wale up to the point of the gap.
3 Work a three-rod border across the gap, using the appropriate weavers from the wale.
4 Continue waling round the basket, using the last three ends from the border stakes.

End Treatments

There are times when a rod border is worked from one side to another, and not continuously around the top of a basket. This could be on the sides of certain types of squarework or across the ends of a square lid. If the border is to be worked on a lid, it will be necessary to trim the centre sticks close to the edge of the weaving but leaving the sticks at the edges. Slype and insert stakes into the weaving in order to work the border.

a) *Method 1, for a three-rod border* (Figs 104/105)

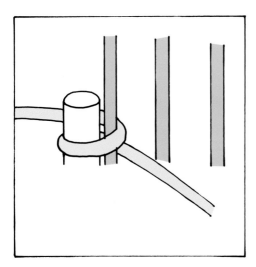

104a Taking an extra rod round the corner post and stake

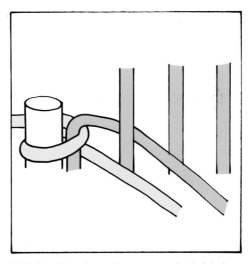

104b Bending down the corner stake behind one

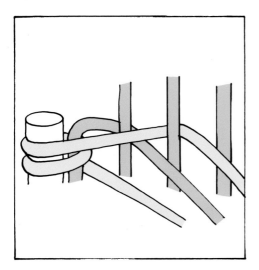

104c Weaving the extra rod in front of one, behind one

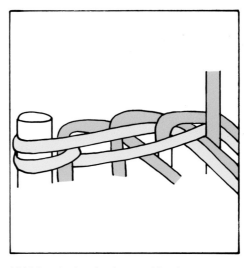

104d Continuing the three-rod border

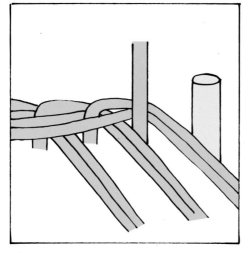

105a Reaching the corner post (Method 1)

105b Kinking and trimming the next rod

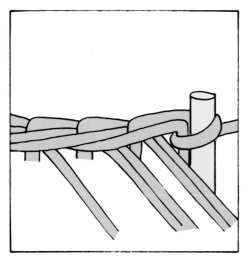

105c Taking the last stake twice round the corner post and cramming off the kinked rod

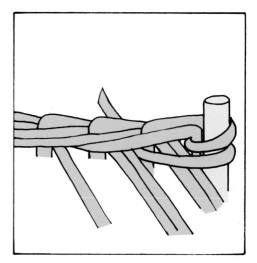

105d Weaving the last stake through to the back

b) *Method 2, for a four-rod-behind-two border* (Figs 106/107)

After the border is completed, the outside posts at each side can be sawn off level.

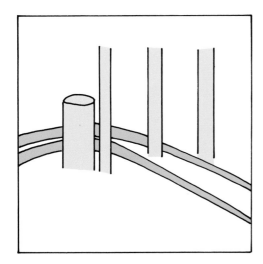

106a Two extra rods put into position

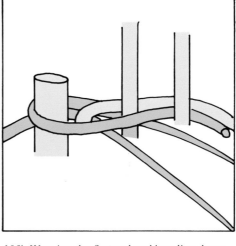

106b Weaving the first rod and bending down the first stake

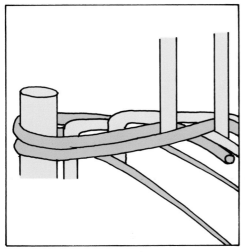

106c Continuing the border

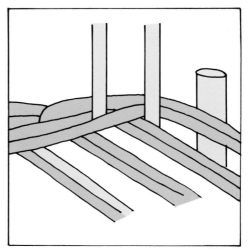

107a Reaching the corner post

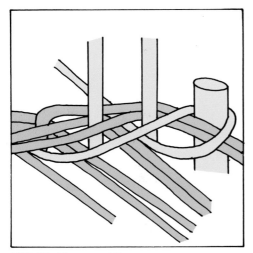

107b Working round the corner

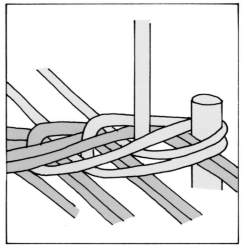

107c Completing the corner, leaving one upright stake as a tie

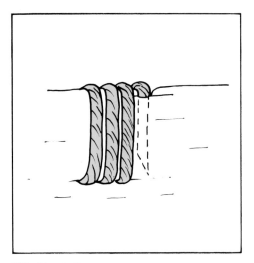

108a Simple tie

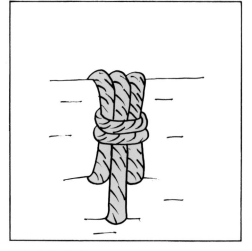

108b Butterfly tie

Ties or Bands

These are used to secure the ends when a border is not continuous.

a) *Simple Tie* (Fig 108a)

1 Insert a slyped butt end beside the first stake from the edge.

2 Twist the rod (see page 43).

3 Wind the twisted rod three times over the back of the border and a few rows of the weaving.

4 Weave the ends away.

b) *Butterfly Tie* (Fig 108b)

1 Insert a slyped butt beside the first stake from the edge.

2 Twist the rod (see page 43).

3 Wind over the border and a few rows of the weaving three times, taking the centre strand down lower into the weaving.

4 Wind the rod twice round the centre.

5 Weave the ends away.

Four x three plait border

109a Working the first pair

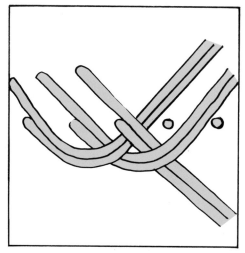

109b Working the second pair

109c Bringing the first pair back to the front
with the next stake

109d Continuing the border

PLAIT BORDER

This is a decorative border, used most often on bowls or trays where there is no handle. The border protrudes quite a way over the sides of the basket, making it bulky to secure a handle.

Simple 3 x 2 Plait Border

1 Choose three extra rods the same thickness as the stakes.
2 Kink two stakes down so that there is enough room for a rod to pass underneath. Lay two of the extra rods beside and to the right of each one.

3 Take the first pair in front of the next upright stake through to the inside of the basket.
4 Bend down the upright stake and lay the third extra rod alongside it (Fig 109a).
5 Take the next pair in front of the next upright stake through to the inside (Fig 109b). Bend the stake over them and bring the first pair (inside the basket) round to the outside alongside it (Fig 109c). Repeat this stage once more.
6 There are now two sets of three rods bent down to the outside. Taking the left-hand two rods each time and leaving the inner one, the stroke is repeated all round the basket (Fig 109d).

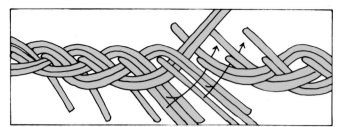

110a Taking the last pairs through to the inside

110b Bringing the three extra stakes through to the outside

110c Bringing the last three ends through to the outside

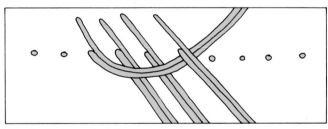

111a Beginning a three-by-two plait worked over more stakes

111b Completed plait

7 To finish the border, thread the last two pairs through to the inside of the basket (Fig 110a).

8 Thread the three extra stakes (butt ends) through to the front (Fig 110b).

9 Take the rod closest to the border of the remaining three pairs and thread through to the outside of the basket (Fig 110c).

10 Trim off three remaining ends on the inside.

11 Cane workers can remove the three extra rods completely and finish the weave by threading the ends through in their place to make the weave complete.

Variations on Plait Borders

There are many variations on the basic plait border. These can be worked by using more extra stakes to make the border thicker or carrying the rods along further during the working of the plait (Fig 111a,b). Once you have mastered the underlying structure, you should be able to work out how to do the variations.

4 x 3 Plait Border

(Figs 112-113).

Plait Border Round a Notch

1 Leave the stakes in the notch standing while the rest of the siding is worked.
2 Slype and insert extra stakes into the stick each side of the notch, using a well greased bodkin to make the space.
3 Work any of the plait borders right round the basket, incorporating the stakes at the bottom and sides of the notch.

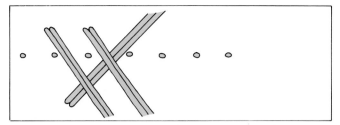

112a Beginning position for six extra rods

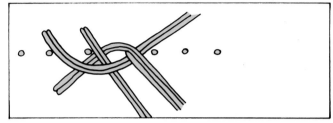

112b Beginning the border

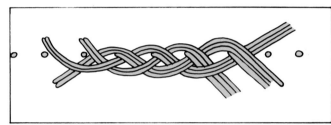

112c Four on the inside, three on the outside

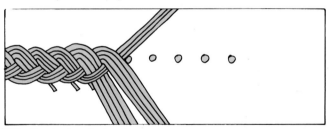

113a Continuing the border

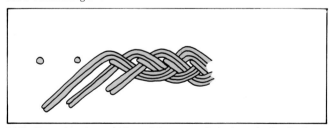

113b Changing the position of the extra six rods at the beginning

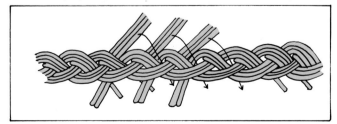

113c Completing the border

114a Border finished on the outside

114b Border finished on the inside

Plait border used as the side of a tray

Plait used as the Side of a Tray

1 Stake up as normal.
2 Place the tray between the knees with the right side facing you.
3 Work the plait border as usual but when reaching the point where a stake is left behind each time, continue with the end of the rod and incorporate it into the next stroke, so that it is left on the far side of the border. (This will be the underneath of the tray) (Fig 114a,b).
4 This method can also be used to make a lid, in which case it is worked with the underside facing the worker, so that the right side becomes the outside of the lid.

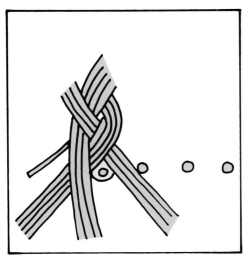

115a Approaching the corner

Dealing with Corners

As with rod borders, change the stroke of the plait around a square corner to make a neater finish. There are two ways to do this: the folded method (Fig 115a,b,c) and the curved method (Fig 116a,b,c,d). Either method can be worked round the corner post. If you wish to cover the corner post, cut it level with the waling and add in an extra stake. (See Rod Borders).

115b Working the corner

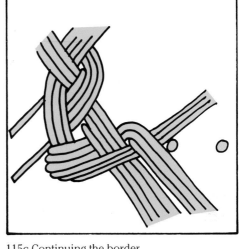

115c Continuing the border

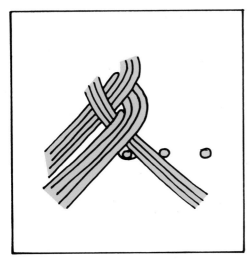

116a Approaching the corner

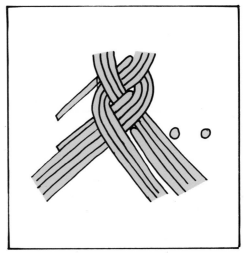

116b Bending the corner stake and taking the rest of the rods alongside

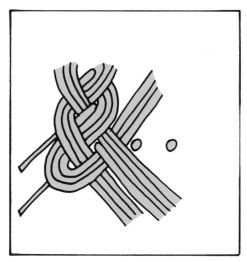

116c Working round the corner

116d Continuing the border

Wrapped border over a core

BORDERS WITH A CORE

A core for a wrapped border can be made with a bunch of thinner material coiled round the edge as a rim, the wrapping holding it into place, or a more solid structure can be made with a thick rod or length of centre cane.

1 Cut a length of centre cane, or a thick piece of willow, long enough to fit around the outside of the border stakes with a good overlap.

2 Make it into a hoop to fit around the outside of the border stakes. Overlap the ends (see Fig 42), glue and nail to hold.

Skeined

1 Kink each stake just above the surface of the weave and bend towards the next stake on the right. Kink again and bend down beside the next stake.

2 Trim off the stakes, allowing enough to slype and insert alongside the next stake (Fig 117a).

3 Using small modelling nails, nail the top of each bent stake to the inside of the hoop (Fig 117b).

4 Use willow skeins or chair seating cane to wrap over the stakes and hoop all the way round the basket.

5 This wrapped border can also be continued into a wrapped handle.

It is also possible to vary the wrapping in more decorative ways by using the techniques for wrapped handles.

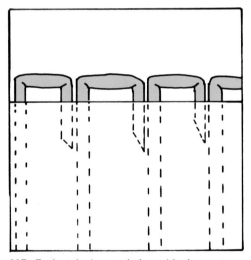

117a Each stake inserted alongside the next

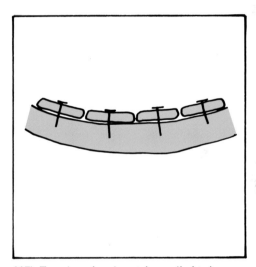

117b Top view showing stakes nailed to hoop

Centre-cane basket with border and handle
wrapped with chair seating cane

Wrapped

1 Work a behind-one trac all round the basket to bring the stakes down to the front.

2 Make a hoop to fit round the basket (Fig 42) and place in position outside the stakes.

3 Take each rod in turn, in front of four stakes, over the core and back through to the front (Fig 118a).

4 Repeat with rounds of wrapping in this way until the entire core is covered (Fig 118b).

5 Thread the ends through to the inside of the basket and trim off neatly.

An alternative method is to work an in-front-of-one trac at the beginning so that the ends are on the inside. Work the wrap in the opposite direction so that the ends finish on the inside. This is more tricky to do but a neater finish.

FOLLOW-ON BORDERS

A follow-on border is used to make the edge firmer and stronger, to create a decorative effect or to form a ledge. Any combination of borders can be used.

Although normally a trac border is slender and not too strong, it is possible to work one or more follow-on tracs to make a much stronger, thicker edge. Another version is to add a follow-on trac after a rod border. Follow-on trac borders can be worked either forwards or backwards (Fig 119a,b).

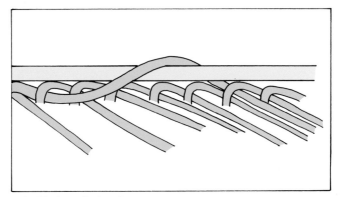

118a Working the border

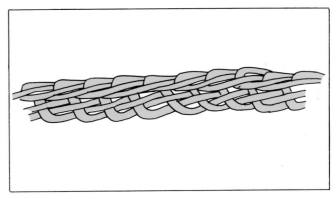

118b Top view of completed border

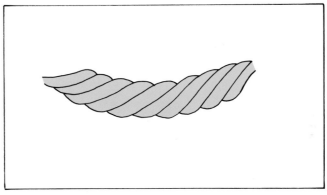

119a Follow-on trac, behind one, in front of one

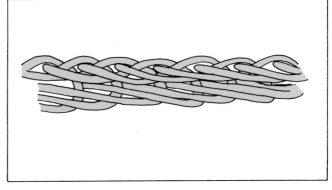

119b Back trac, in front of two

If a border is required to rest on the side rather than on the top of the basket, work a simple trac before the main border follows on. This is often used when a handle is required with a plait border. Since the plait normally protrudes quite a way beyond the edge of the basket, working the plait flat onto the sides makes it easier to accommodate the handle.

FOOT BORDERS

These are borders added onto the base of a basket to make an extra firm rim on which the basket stands and to lift the base of the basket off the ground to save on wear and spoiling. A foot border can sometimes be used to disguise an uneven base and can be replaced if it wears out.

If a basket is to have a foot border, the first round of the upsett must be a three-rod wale starting with tips. While normally the first round would be worked tightly to the underside of the basket to hide the 'elbows' of the pricked-up stakes, the wale must here be worked straight onto the side, leaving them exposed.

Work the foot border (after the top border) by turning the basket upside down, and insert stakes down into the siding, alongside the original stakes. Then weave a few rows of waling and turn down a border.

TWISTED ROPE BORDER AND HANDLE

Although this technique can be used just to work a border, it is normally done so that the handle is incorporated into it.

1 Add an extra stake each side of two adjacent stakes in the centre of each side (Fig 120a).
2 Place the basket between the knees. Take the first three handle weavers (top left) and , without kinking the rods, twist them clockwise with the right hand to form a three-strand rope (Fig 120b).

3 Place the twisted weavers between the two sets of handle weavers on the opposite side in a loop which forms the handle bow (Fig 120c).
4 Turn the basket round, repeat the twist with the second group, then take them under the handle bow three times (Fig 120d).
5 Turn the basket again and work in the same way with group three and group four, to form a thick rope handle made up of four twisted groups of three rods.
6 Take the left-hand group, twist it clockwise through to the inside of the basket underneath the right-hand group (Fig 121a).
7 Continue in this way, incorporating one stake with each group coming from inside to outside (Fig 121b). Work round the basket, leaving the shortest end on the inside at each stroke.
8 Work round the handle end on the other side, incorporating the other two groups of weavers as well. This will entail dropping extra weavers to keep the border even.
9 Complete the border by threading the remaining ends into the border at the beginning.

Twisted-rope border and handle (worked together)

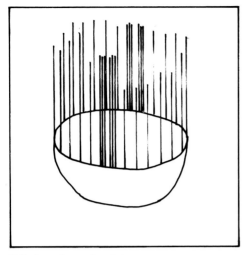

120a Inserting extra stakes

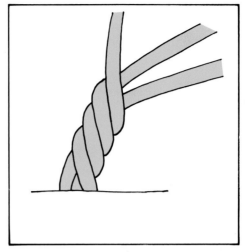

120b Twisting the rods

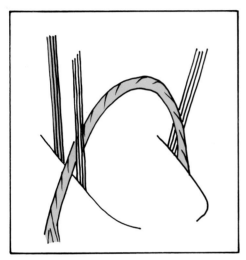

120c Forming the handle bow

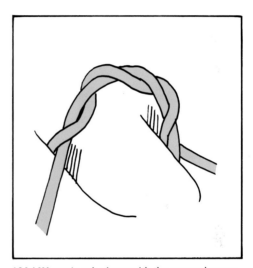

120d Wrapping the bow with the second group of rods

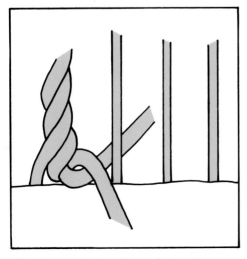

121a Working the handle into the border

121b Continuing the border

Simple basket with four-rod border and follow-
on trac

Chapter 8
HANDLES

There are basically three types of handle: large handles which reach across a basket, small handles which are worked into the sides (as in a log basket) and handles made entirely separately and attached afterwards. Another possibility is to leave a space in the weaving to act as a hand hold just under the border.

BOW HANDLES

These are handles which go across a basket in a loop (eg a shopping basket). They require a bow or core to be inserted before working the handle. A handle bow can either be inserted directly into the siding after the basket has been made, thus holding it very firmly in place, or a space can be allowed for it during the weaving. The latter is less inclined to distort the basket. You will need handle liners to hold the space open until the weaving and the border are completed.

Handle Liners

These can be made in two ways, in both cases put into position after the upsett.

a) Cut pieces from the butt ends of thick willows, long enough to reach from the upsett to the border plus a good bit spare to make them easy to remove. Slype the tip ends, and place alongside a stake at the handle position, or use one or more

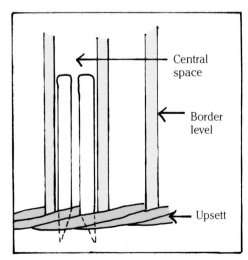

122a Single handle-liner   122b Double handle-liners

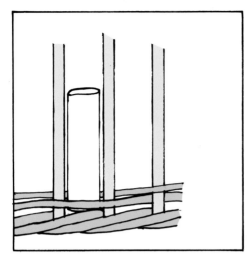

123 Slat used as handle liner

between two stakes where a very thick handle with one or more bows is to be used (Fig 122a,b).
b) Slats can be used to hold open the space between two stakes throughout the weaving of the sides (Fig 123) and are removed before working the border. This method is often used where there is to be a bridge.

The Handle Bow

The handle bow may consist of one or more rods, depending on the weight and look of the basket. If two or three rods are used, alternate butts and tips and ensure that they are exactly the same height and lie smoothly alongside each other.

1 On a round basket, align the handle with either of the central base sticks.
2 To find the correct position for a handle bow, use a measure to find the centre and insert a well greased bodkin into the appropriate place on each side. This will be alongside the nearest stake, if the handle is to be inserted directly into the sides without using handle liners.
3 Cut the bow from a well mellowed stout rod 8-10ft (240-300cm) long, enough to make the handle, and reach

well down into the weaving on each side. A common mistake for beginners is to make the bow too long. The handle must be in proportion to the rest of the basket.
4 Slype both ends on the belly side and ease the bow over the thumbs to shape.
5 Insert the bow into the prepared channel, pushing well down but not allowing too much pressure to kink the bow.

Handle Rods

Choosing rods of suitable thickness for covering a particular handle is important, requiring experience and understanding of the particular method used. If in doubt try to measure against rods in a similar handle on another basket.

Rope Handle

1 Choose ten slender rods of equal thickness, long enough to reach across the handle bow with about 15in (38cm) to spare.
2 Insert four rods at each end, around and to the left of the handle bow (Fig 124a).
3 Take the four rods on one side over the handle bow three times, avoiding kinks and not allowing the rods to cross each other (Fig 124b). The method of finishing will dictate whether the rods are left on the inside or the outside of the basket.
4 Work the four rods on the other side of the basket in the same way, filling in the gaps left by the first four.
5 It is important that the handle bow is covered evenly without overlapping the rods to cause bumps or leaving grins. If there are large spaces in the wrapping, one or both of the remaining rods can be inserted beside the other and used to fill the gaps.
6 If the handle has been unevenly wrapped so that there are grins on top and crowding underneath, turn the basket upside down and tap the underside of the handle with a rapping iron to even them out.

124a Placing the rods around the handle bow

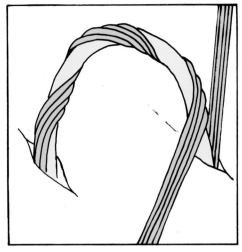

124b Wrapping three times over the handle

Rope Handle Finishes

Method a)

1 Having left the wrapping rods on the inside of the basket, thread them through to the outside, under the border or through the waling to the left of the handle bow.

2 Take the ends together, around the handle (Fig 125a), across themselves and thread them through to the inside of the basket, under the border to the opposite side of the handle (Fig 125b).

3 Weave the ends away by weaving in and out of the waling a couple of times, then trim them.

4 Repeat on the other side of the basket.

125a Taking the rods across and round behind the handle bow

125b Crossing them over themselves and through to the inside

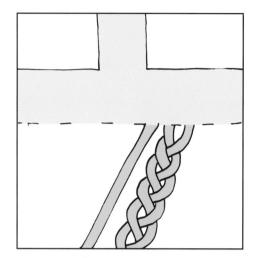

126a Plaiting three of the rods

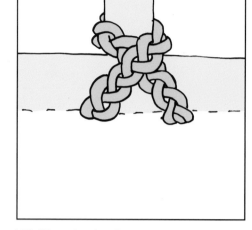

126b Wrapping the plait round the handle

Method b)

1 Having left the wrapping rods on the inside of the basket, thread them through to the outside, to the left of the handle bow.

2 Take three of the rods and braid them into a plait long enough to go around the handle (Fig 126a), back over itself and thread under the border to the inside of the basket, to the opposite side of the handle bow (Fig 126b).

3 Weave the ends away securely, including the spare wrapping rod, then trim them.

4 Repeat on the other side of the basket.

Detail of the herringbone effect of method C, used to finish a rope handle

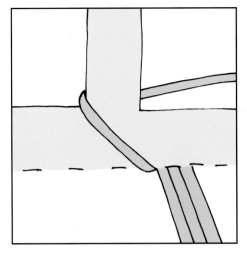

127a Taking the first rod round the handle

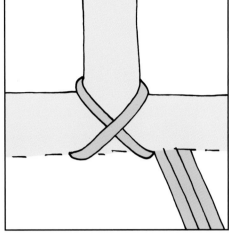

127b Threading it through to the inside

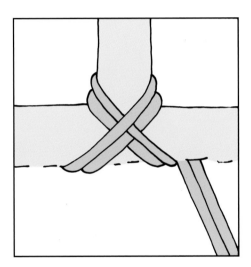

127c Repeating with the second rod

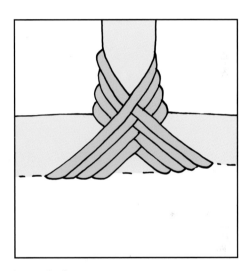

127d The crossings completed

Method c)

1 Having left the wrapping rods on the inside of the basket thread them through to the outside, to the left of the handle bow.

2 Starting with the rod nearest the handle bow, take each in turn around the handle (Fig 127a), across itself and thread through to the inside of the basket, under the border to the opposite side of the handle (Fig 127b). Make sure that each rod lies above its predecessor without crossing over at the back and keep the rods pulled tightly into position for a really neat finish (Fig 127c,d).

3 Weave the ends away and trim off.

4 Repeat on the other side of the basket.

128a Threading the rods through to the inside

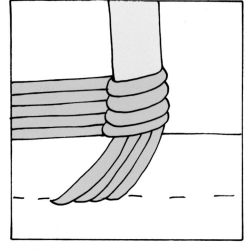

128b Wrapping them round the handle

Method d)

1 Having left the wrapping rods on the outside of the basket, thread them through to the inside, to the left of the handle bow (Fig 128a).

2 Bring the wrapping rods straight up and over to the front. Pull tightly round the handle to the front again (Fig 128b), then thread under the beginning and through to the inside of the basket (Fig 128c).

3 Weave the ends away and trim off.

4 Repeat on the other side of the basket.

128c Threading them through the beginning and to the inside

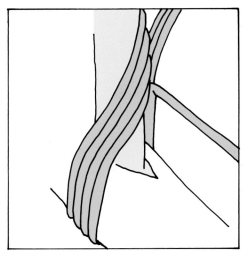

129a Rods folded up and wrapping end kinked

129b Ends folded down over first wrap

Method e)

1 Having left the wrapping rods on the outside of the basket, thread them through to the inside, to the left of the handle bow.

2 Fold up the threads along the underside of the handle bow and hold.

3 The wrapping can be done with one of these rods or if they are too fine add in an extra one for the purpose (Fig 129a).

4 Kink the rod about 1in (2.5cm) up from the border.

5 The rod can be used as it is, but it can also be twisted before continuing, to make it stronger.

6 Wrap this rod once round the handle, then fold the remaining ends down over it (Fig 129b).

7 Continue wrapping downwards towards the border (Fig 129c).

8 To finish, make a channel with a bodkin through the handle bow and pull the end tightly through.

9 The wrapping can be started off at the bottom and worked up the handle before being finished in the same way. In this case the ends are trimmed off, not folded over.

129c Wrapping completed

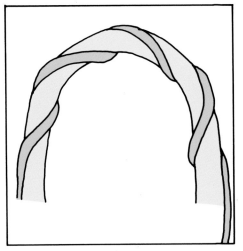

130a First twisted rod worked five times round the handle

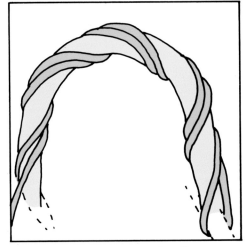

130b Working back across the handle

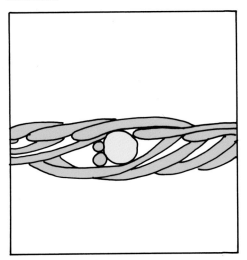

130c Placing the third rod

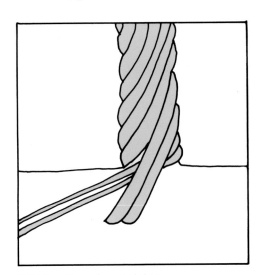

130d Two tip ends remaining

Twisted Rope Handle

1 Choose four rods of equal thickness, long enough to reach across the handle bow twice with about 8in (20cm) to spare.

2 Slype and insert one rod beside and to the left of the handle bow, then twist it.

3 Holding the basket between the knees, wind the twisted rod over the handle bow five times from left to right, ending on the outside (Fig 130a).

4 Take the weaver through to the inside of the basket, under the border, to the left of the handle and work back across the handle bow to the beginning, keeping the twist even (Fig 130b). Push the tip

temporarily into the side of the basket to hold.

5 Slype and insert the second weaver on the opposite side of the basket. Twist it and wrap across the handle, placing the rod in between the two already there and back again.

6 Insert the third weaver to the inside of the first (Fig 130c) and twist it. Wrap over the handle, across to the other side and back, working it in between the weavers to keep it in the correct channel.

7 Work the fourth weaver as the third but on the opposite side of the basket.

8 There are now two tip ends on the outside of each side of the basket (Fig 130d). Twist these two ends together.

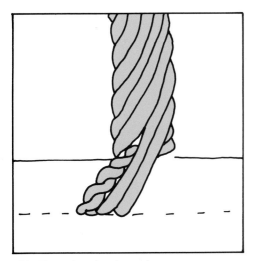

131a Tip ends twisted together

131b Twisted tips wrapped around the handle

9 Thread them under the border to the inside and weave the ends away (Fig 131a).

10 If the tip ends are long enough, it makes a neater finish to take the twisted pair around the handle before taking them through to the inside (Fig 131b).

Twisted rope handle

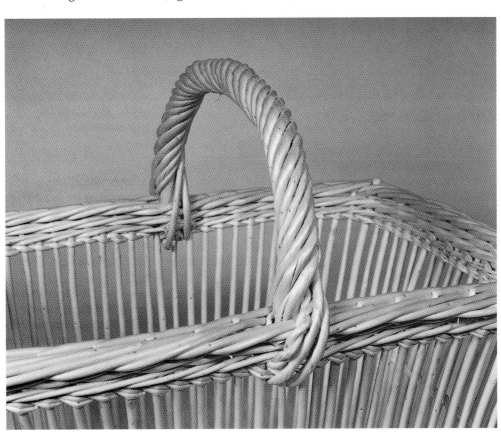

Wrapped Handle

White-willow oval shopping basket with skein-wrapped handle and base sticks

Skeins or chair seating cane can be very effectively used as wrapping for handles. (For how to make skeins see page 41). The three parts of a wrapped handle are the bow (or core), the leader and the wrapping itself. A leader is necessary to hold the wrapping tight and stop it slipping. It can be one or more fine rods or skeins, long enough to reach across the handle.

1 Insert one or more handle bows.
2 Lay in the leader, by pushing it into the side of the basket on top of the handle bow (Fig 132a).
3 Attach the wrapping skein to the base of the handle and around the border (Fig 132b).

4 Make a few wraps round the handle, then work under and over the leader in a regular pattern (Fig 132c).
5 Fancy wrapped handles can use more leaders or have extra skeins wrapped over the leader (Fig 133a,b). This is known as listing.
6 To make a join, insert the new end between the wrapping and the underside of the handle, with its shiny side against the handle. Cross the two ends and continue with the new end, wrapping over the old (Fig 134).
7 Finish off at the other end to match the beginning. Weave the end away securely (a dab of glue is useful).

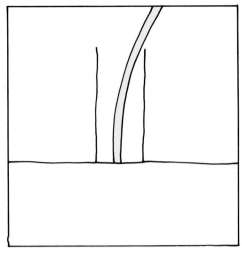

132a Laying in the leader

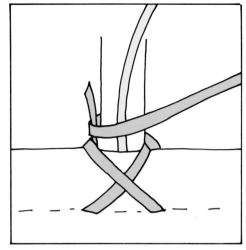

132b Crossing the handle to start

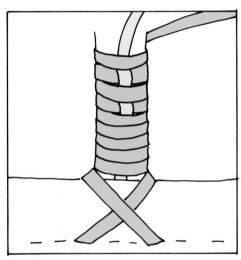

132c Beginning the wrapping

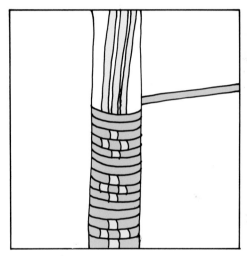

133a Extra leaders

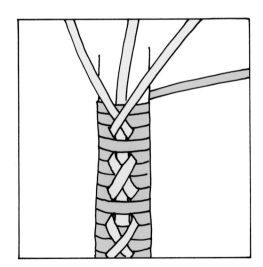

133b Listing

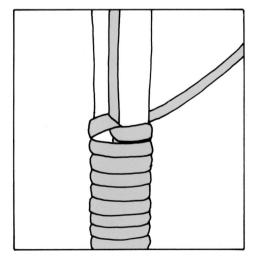

134 Joining

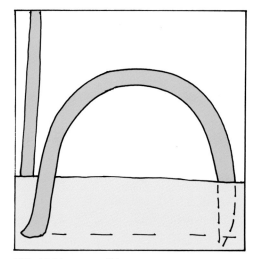

135a Making a small bow

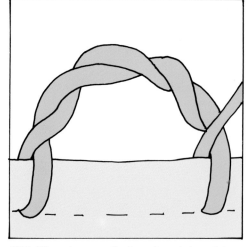

135b Wrapping over the bow from left to right

SMALL TWISTED HANDLES

Simple One-Rod Twisted Handle

This can be used on small items, either into the siding or onto the edge of a tray, for example.

1 Insert a slyped rod alongside a stake (or stick if on a lid). Twist the rod.
2 Make a small bow and thread the rod through to the inside of the basket (Fig 135a).
3 Keeping the twist, wind back over the bow, to form a rope effect as the two strands intertwine (Fig 135b).
4 Thread from outside to inside the basket and back again across the handle, making three strands to the rope (Fig 135c).
5 Weave the end away.

135c Wrapping over the bow from right to left to complete the 'rope'

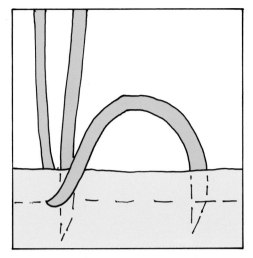

136a Forming the bow

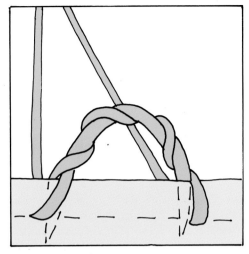

136b First wrapping

136c Second wrapping

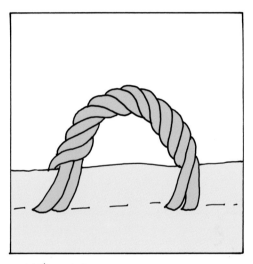

136d Completed handle

TWO-ROD TWISTED HANDLE

This handle is most commonly seen on log baskets. There are many variations on the way it can be worked, although the general principle is the same. This version is worked from the outside of the basket.

1 Slype and insert two stout rods a hand's width apart into the siding alongside two stakes. The right-hand rod must be the thicker of the two, as it will form the bow.

2 Make the bow (enough to accommodate a hand), taking the right-hand rod over to the left of the other rod and from the outside to the inside of the basket (Fig 136a).

3 Twist the second rod (see page 43) and wind under the handle three times.

4 Thread under the border to the inside and right of the bow (Fig 136b). Wind over again to the left and through to the inside (Fig 136c).

5 Twist the remainder of the first rod and wind across, under the handle and back in the same way (Fig 136d).

6 Any gaps can be filled with the remainder of the tip ends.

7 Thread the ends away.

Two-Rod Twisted Handle onto a Lid

1 Straight cut on the belly side of the butt end of two rods, one slightly thicker than the other, to form the bow.

2 Make a space with a greased bodkin into the weaving of the lid beside the lid sticks. Insert the rods, kink 1in (2.5cm) back along the rod and tap into place (Fig 137a).

3 Form the thicker rod into a bow and thread through to the underside of the lid.

4 Twist the second rod, wind over the bow three times and thread through to the underside.

5 Continue as for a handle worked into the siding but place a stout stick underneath the lid and work the handle over it (Fig 137b).

6 If there is a central stick, it is possible to work the handle without adding an extra stick.

Two-rod twisted handle onto a lid

Two-rod twisted handle

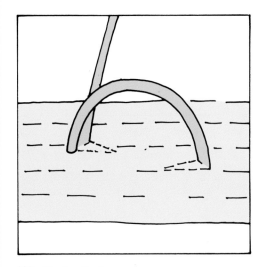

137a Placing the bow

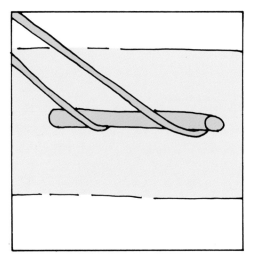

137b Underneath the lid, working over a stick

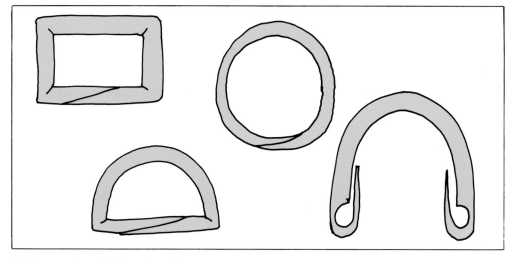

138 Separate handles in various shapes

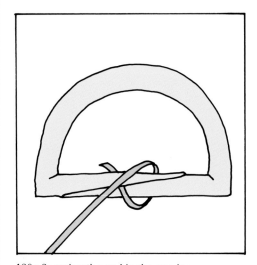

139a Securing the end in the overlap

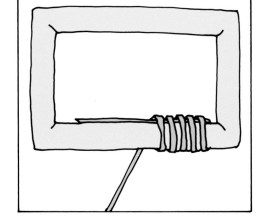

139b Securing the end under the wrapping

ATTACHED HANDLES

Wrapped

It is relatively simple to make handles of various shapes in the same way as making a hoop for a base (Fig 138). These can be wrapped decoratively in the same way as a wrapped bow handle (see Figs 132-4). The handle can then be attached to the basket with a twisted rod (see page 43).

There are two ways to begin the wrapping on this type of handle.

a) Thread the skein into the overlap, wrap to secure the join, then continue around the handle (Fig 139a).
b) Fold the skein along the underside of the handle and wrap over it (Fig 139b).

Complete the wrapping to the chosen design. To finish off, loosen the last few wraps, thread the end back through it and then tighten.

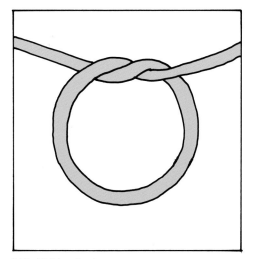

140a Making the loop

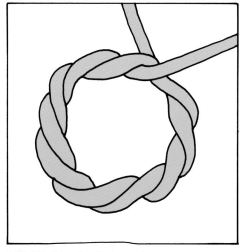

140b Working the first round

140c Trimming the ends on the underside

Simple Loops

1 Choose a well mellowed, fine rod and loop round into a ring (Fig 140a).

2 Take the tip end three or four times over the ring (Fig 140b), until you reach the beginning.

3 Repeat to form a three-strand 'rope'.

4 Trim the ends on the inside of the hoop (Fig 140c).

Chapter 9
LIDS, FASTENINGS AND FITTINGS

ROUND AND OVAL LIDS

Lids for round and oval baskets can be approached in various ways. They can be flat or convex and with or without a handle or loop. They can also be held in place by a ledge on the basket or a flange on the lid (Fig 141). It is very important to measure carefully to make sure that the lid will fit the basket.

Resting on an Inner Ledge

1 Make the lid like a base, keeping the joins on the underside.
2 Stake up as if for sides, then turn down a border straight onto the edge. Hold the lid between the knees to work the border, otherwise it becomes very difficult to control.

Resting on an Outer Ledge

1 Make the lid like a base, keeping the joins on the underside.
2 Stake up and prick up as if for sides, weave an upsett and then turn down a border.

See also plait border used as side of a tray page 118.

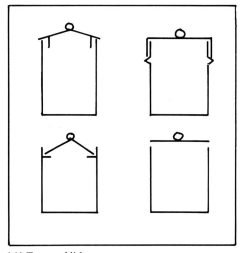

141 Types of lids

Lid with an Inner Flange

1 Make the lid like a base, keeping the joins on the underside, but work only until it measures to within ½in (1cm) of the inner edge of the basket border.
2a Stake up and work a trac border with the ends on the inside. Work a follow-on trac with the tip ends to make a flange (Fig 142a).
2b Alternatively, stake up, prick up and weave the inner flange, and turn down a border. Then continue weaving to the edge of the lid, stake up again and turn down a border on the edge (Fig 142b).

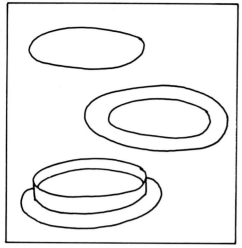

142a Working the border first then the flange

142b Working the flange first then the border

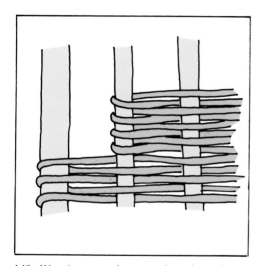

143a Weaving up to the second notch mark

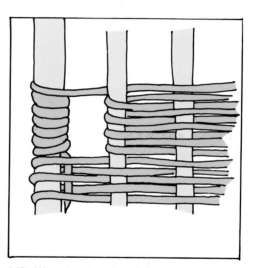

143b Wrapping the edge stick

SQUARE LIDS

Square lids are also worked in a similar way to bases. Whichever method is used, measuring is vital to ensure that the lid fits properly. It will be necessary to turn down a border on each end (see page 111).

When working a square lid in a screw block, there is a natural tendency for the work to curve away from the worker. It is better to make all the joins on the side facing you and make this the underside of the lid. This will have the effect of making it lie flatter on the basket.

Notch

A notch is a space left at the edge of a lid to accommodate fastenings or hinges.

1 Use single outside sticks and mark the position for the notch.
2 Weave up to the first notch mark.
3 Continue weaving across the lid, excluding the outside stick as far as the second notch mark (Fig 143a).
4 Insert a slyped rod into the weaving beside the outside stick, wind it tightly round the stick up to the second notch mark, then weave it across the lid (Fig 143b).
5 Complete the rest of the lid as normal.

Shopping basket with U-shaped lids attached
to a bridge

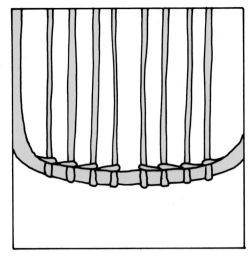

144a Scalloming in two directions

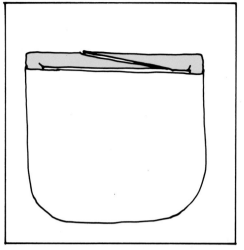

144b Overlapping the outer posts

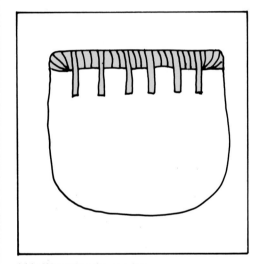

144c Wrapping the overlap

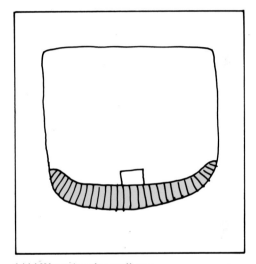

144d Wrapping the scalloms

U-SHAPED LIDS

When working a scallomed U-shaped lid, the scalloms can be attached in both directions to leave a central space for a fastening (Fig 144a). The ends can be either bordered down like the end of a square lid or the outside posts can be overlapped and wrapped as follows.

1 Trim the inner sticks.
2 Kink or prick down the outer posts towards each other.
3 Shave the ends to make a neat overlap (Fig 144b).
4 Wrap with skeins or chair cane, making an extra wrap into the weave every few turns to secure it (Fig 144c).
5 The scallomed end can also be wrapped for a very neat finish (Fig 144d).

145a Inside ledge

145b Outside ledge

LEDGES

Inside Ledge for Round and Oval Baskets (Fig 145a)

1 Work a trac border, leaving the ends on the inside.
2 Work a follow-on trac with the remaining ends to form a ledge around the inside, just below the original border.

Outside Ledge for Round and Oval Baskets (Fig 145b)

1 Work a trac border, leaving the ends on the outside.
2 Work a follow-on trac with the remaining ends to form a ledge around the outside of the basket, just below the original border.

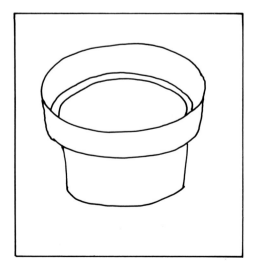

145c Inner ledge with raised border

Raised Border to Form an Inner Ledge (Fig 145c)

1 Work a three-rod border.
2 Take each end under one stake to the right and bend upright.
3 Wale for a few rounds, starting and finishing with tips.
4 Turn down a three-rod border. The original border forms the ledge.

Corner Ledge for a Drop-in Tray

Although this can be done after the basket is made, it is easier to do during the weaving of the sides of the basket.

1 Slype both ends of pieces cut from the butt ends of four rods.
2 Kink the slyped pieces about 2in (5cm) from each end.
3 Insert the ends into the weaving at each side of a corner, at a suitable height for a drop-in tray (Fig 145d).

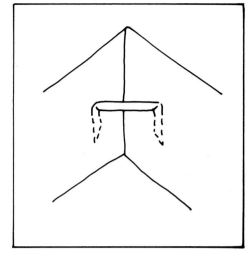

145d Corner ledge

FASTENINGS

Twisting and Plaiting

These techniques can be used as a small loop at the centre of a round lid, as well as being useful in a wide range of fastenings.

Two Twisted Rods

1 Take one fine rod and fold it in half round a stake.
2 Twist the right-hand section clockwise a couple of times before laying it across the left-hand rod.
3 Change hands and repeat until the required length is reached (Fig 146a).

Three Plaited Rods

1 Take two fine rods. Insert one with a slyped butt into the weaving, then fold the other in half round a stake.
2 With these three ends, braid tightly for the required length (Fig 146b).

146a Two-strand twist

146b Three-strand plait

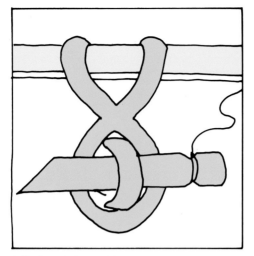

147a Simple looped fastening

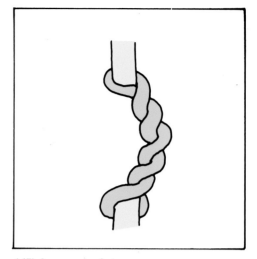

147b Loop on basket

Simple Looped Fastening
(Fig 147a)

1 Make a twisted two-strand loop on to a side stake and weave the ends away (Fig 147b).

2 Make another twisted two-strand loop onto the edge of the lid. This must be long enough to reach across and round the loop on the basket.

3 Thread one strand back through the twist and continue twisting together up to the edge of the lid (Fig 147c).

4 Wrap once over the edge stick and weave the ends away.

5 Use a straight, slyped butt end of a stout rod as a peg.

6 Cut a small channel around the other end of the peg and attach to the basket with a single twisted rod or a thong.

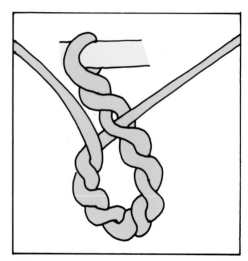

147c Loop on lid

Plaited Loops and Stick (Fig 148a)

1 When making the lid, allow for two holes in appropriate places.

2 Work a plait into the border of the basket, with one rod inserted beside a stake and one looped through the border. Thread back through the border and weave the ends away (Fig 148b).

3 Use a long, straight stick cut from the butt end or a piece of dowelling to thread through the loops.

148a Plaited loops and stick

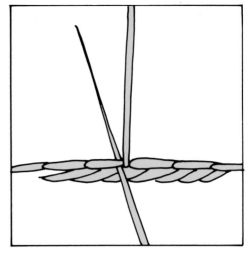

148b Beginning the plait

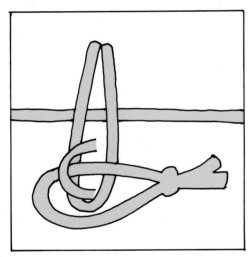

149a Loop and toggle

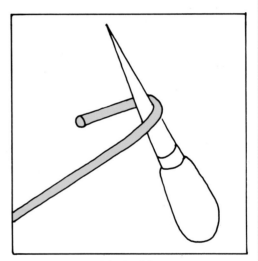

149b Easing round the bodkin

Loop and Toggle (Fig 149a)

1 Make a small twisted or plaited loop onto the basket.
2 Make a longer loop onto the lid, long enough to reach round the first loop.
3 Make a toggle through the first loop by easing a piece of willow around a bodkin handle (Fig 149b), then tying the tip end into a knot (Fig 149c).

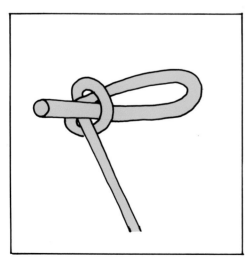

149c Making the toggle

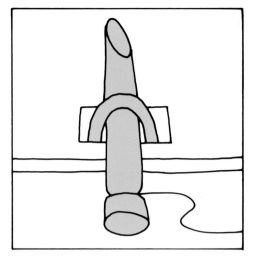

150 Loop and peg

151 Leather strap

Loop and Peg (Fig 150)

1 Make the lid with a space at the centre front.
2 Work a loop onto the border to fit into the space.
3 Make a peg from a piece cut from a thick butt end.
4 Attach the peg to the basket with a twisted rod or a thong.

Leather Straps (Fig 151)

If leather straps are to be used to fasten the basket, a notch must be left at an appropriate place on the lid.

HINGES

There are many variations on the methods used to make hinges; some are stronger than others, and the technique will also change depending on whether the attachment is edge-to-edge or overlapping (Fig 152a,b).

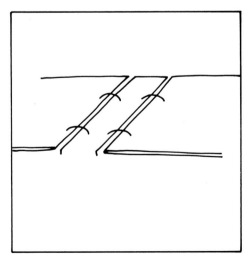

152a Edge-to-edge hinge

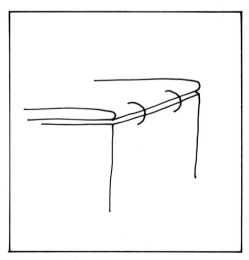

152b Overlapping hinge

153 Lashed hinge

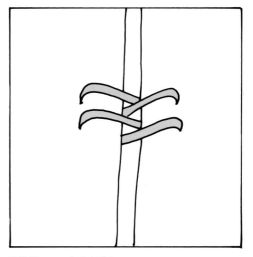

154 Figure-of-eight hinge

Lashed Hinge

This method can be done with a twisted rod or a length of thonging. Insert the twisted rod into the border and wrap over both the edge stick on the lid and the border for the length of the side (Fig 153).

Figure-of-Eight Hinge

Work this with a twisted rod where the lid is edge to edge (Fig 154).

Simple Twisted Hinge

1 Insert a rod into the border and twist.
2 Keeping the tension on the twist, thread through from inside to outside under the border.
3 At this point, rub a little tallow on the rod to stop the hinges from squeaking and to help preserve them.
4 Thread through the top of the lid, over the edge stick and back under the border twice.
5 Thread the end through the wraps and knot to secure (Fig 155).

155 Simple twisted hinge

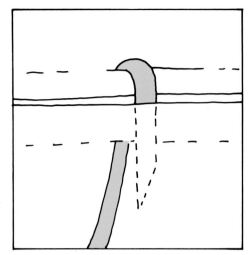

156a Threading over lid and border

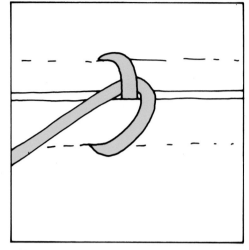

156b Threading behind the first wrap

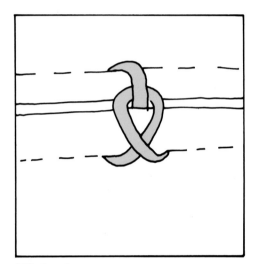

156c Forming a cross

Hinge for Flowed Sides

This hinge holds the lid slightly inside the border, which works well on a basket with flowed sides where the hinge is on the outside edge, not the bridge.

1 Insert a slyped rod into the border and twist.
2 Thread over the edge stick of the lid and through under the border, to the left of the twisted rod (Fig 156a).
3 Cross over the butt and thread the end behind the top of the rod from right to left, at the point where it emerges from the border (Fig 156b).
4 Cross the rod in front of itself from left to right, thread through to the inside of the basket and weave the end away (Fig 156c).

157a Hinging onto a bridge

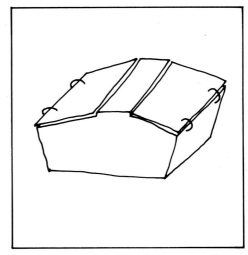

157b Hinging into a border

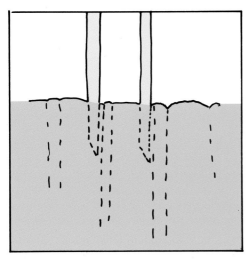

158a Bridge spanning two stakes

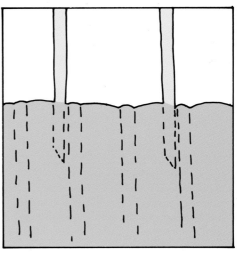

158b Bridge spanning three stakes

FITTINGS

Bridge

A bridge is used where the basket is to have two lids, which can either be hinged onto the bridge itself or the borders (Fig 157a,b). It will be worked after the border and then tied into place by the handle. Unless the bridge is to be very wide it only needs two sticks.

1a Slype and insert two sturdy rods down through the border and into the weaving at the appropriate point. This may span two or three stakes (Fig 158 a,b).

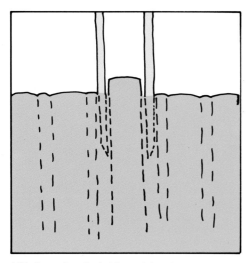

158c Inserting the bridge sticks alongside a slat

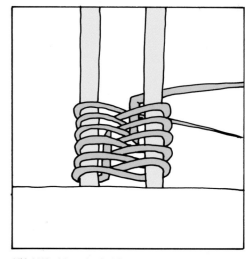

158d Working the bridge

1b Alternatively, leave a space in the weaving of the sides between the two central stakes on each side of the basket. Use a slat to keep the space open and weave in front of and behind the two central stakes. Work the border, then insert the bridge sticks on either side of the slat (Fig 158c).

2 Using fine waste material, beginning with a butt end weave in a figure of eight pattern around the two rods.

3 Weave over the butt at the beginning and insert each new butt into the weaving (Fig 158d).

4 When the correct length is reached, slype and kink the strong rods and insert them at the appropriate place on the other side of the basket.

5 Remove the slat, if used, then work the handle as required.

Leagues

A league is a continuous rod which is laid in across the base and alongside two stakes on opposite sides of the basket. It is used for extra strength and, on very large baskets, leagues are often made of strong wire. Wire leagues can also be looped over a lid and back down into the sides to form a hinge.

DIVISIONS

Divisions are used on all shapes of baskets, and worked on the same principle throughout. The instructions that follow are for single crossed divisions. More complex divisions, such as a twelve-bottle basket, require two screw blocks unless the seated method is used.

Quick Twisted Divisions

1 Thread a sturdy weaver around a stake on the inside of the basket, near to the top.
2 Twist them together to the other side of the basket and secure by weaving the ends away.
3 Work another twisted rod at right angles to the first, as far as the centre.
4 Thread one end through the first, twist and continue to the other side (Fig 159).
5 Secure by weaving the ends away.

Fitched Divisions

1 Measure the basket carefully to find out the length of the sticks required for the divisions. Choose strong, straight rods and cut to size. Since the spaces between the rods will be the same as the thickness, the number needed will depend on the size of the rods. One stick fewer will be required for the second set.
2 Fitch one set of sticks across at the centre and at both ends (Fig 160a).
3 Thread the cross sticks through the middle fitch of the first set (Fig 160b).
4 Fitch both ends of the second set.

159 Quick twisted divisions

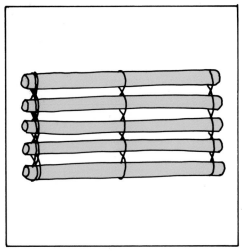

160a First division

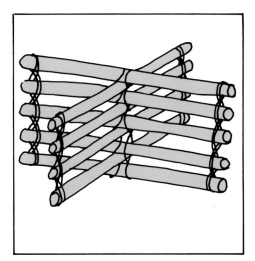

160b Divisions joined together

Woven Partitions

1 Ascertain the length of the partition and cut the sticks to size.

2 Using the screwblock or seated method, work the first partition like a square base, with single sticks on the edges.

3 Make the second partition in the same way but stop weaving about ½in (1cm) before the centre is reached.

4 Pierce the outside sticks of the first panel and thread through the outside sticks of the unfinished panel. Push the inner sticks through the weaving where convenient, preferably all the same side of the stakes of the finished panel (Fig 161).

5 Either sit on or clamp into a screwblock the woven half of the second panel and weave the remainder of the side.

6 Attach the partitions in the same way as the fitched divisions.

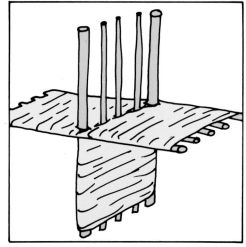

161 Pierced woven partitions

Non-Pierced Woven Partitions

1 Ascertain the length of the partition and cut four sticks to size.

2 Using screwblock or seated method, weave the first partition round two sticks (Fig 162a).

3 Make the second division smaller, narrower by the thickness of two sticks (Fig 162b). Weave to about ½in (1cm) of the centre.

4 Thread the second partition through the weaving of the first at the centre.

5 & 6 (As for woven partitions above.)

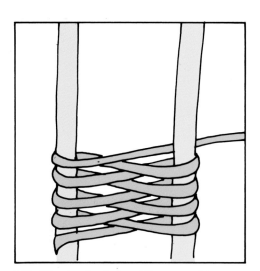

162a Weaving the first partition around two sticks

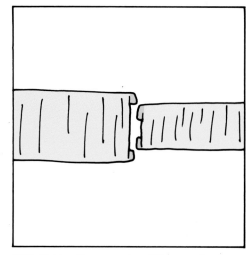

162b Making the second partition smaller by two sticks' width

Four-bottle basket with fitched divisions

Basket designed to hold nine glasses, with non-pierced woven divisions

ATTACHING PARTITIONS

Method 1

1 Place the divisions into the basket.
2 Insert a slyped rod through the basket beside the lowest division stick. Twist. Thread through the basket, around the fitch and back to the outside, working up the basket to the border (Fig 163).
3 Weave the end away.
4 Repeat on all four sides.

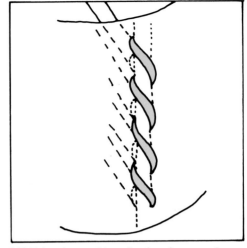

163 Tying the partitions in place by wrapping around a stake on the outside of the basket

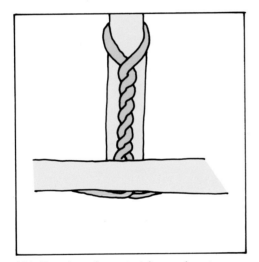

164a Top view of two-strand rope along top stick of division.

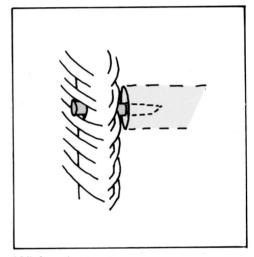

164b Inserting a peg

Method 2

1 Place the partitions inside the basket.
2 Thread a rod through the top stick of the division and twist into a two-strand rope to reach as far as the side of the basket (Fig 164a).
3 Thread through the side of the basket and weave the ends away in opposite directions.
4 Make a channel through the appropriate stake into the end of the outside sticks of the divisions. Insert a peg made from a piece of willow (Fig 164b).

Chapter 10
PROGRAMME OF WORK

Whatever your present level of skill and however large or small the amount of time that you are prepared to put in to learning to make baskets, you will progress more easily by working through a logical programme of work. Good results can only be achieved by getting the basics right first. For instance, the beginner's first round base is bound to be less than perfect. Understandably, the keen student will want to finish his first basket and stand back to admire, but by the time sides, borders and handles have been added, the memory of how the base was made has faded. This is not so much the technique as the 'feel' of it; how fingers work to shape, tighten and even out, to produce a good workable beginning.

It is essential to get enough practice at each stage. It is very tempting to rush ahead with each new technique but, without sufficient experience of what has gone before, very little will have been learnt.

The ideal is to work in multiples of ten. By number five, the technique will have been learnt and any problems ironed out so that by the tenth there should be at least five serviceable bases with which to continue the next stage.

The very best way to learn is under the tuition of an experienced basketmaker. It is not just the techniques, which can be followed from books, but the feel of the material, the pressure from fingers and thumbs, the use of hands, arms, knees etc. This is particularly important at the beginning; it is hard to unlearn bad habits at a later stage.

If you are a complete beginner, start by choosing and sorting materials. Basically, the thickest will be the bottom sticks and the thinnest will be the base weavers. The second thickest will be the side stakes, and in between these and the base weavers will be the side weavers. As a rough guide for cane workers the sizes might be as follows, No 10 for bottom sticks, No 3 for base weaving, No 8 for side stakes and No 5 for side weaving. (See Basics & Special Techniques page 38.)

The importance of choosing the correct materials will be realised as soon as work commences. If the bottom sticks are too thin, the base will have no strength; if they are too thick, the fine base weavers will have difficulty controlling the opening out of the sticks. If the side weavers are thicker than the side stakes, they will take control and instead of weaving in front and behind the stakes the weaving will go straight round while

the stakes are pushed inside and outside. An easy guide would be to have a basket to copy, not for the design but for the size in relation to materials, bearing in mind that very small work is as difficult for the beginner as is very large work.

The following programme has been worked out, beginning with the basics and working up to the more difficult techniques. Having said that, it is much better to keep working on a particular stage until you have mastered it before going on to the next level. If you cannot bring yourself to do ten of everything, we strongly recommend that you work through at least three before going any further.

If you persevere and work through the programme you will discover how infinite the variations are and should be able to start designing your own baskets. The following list covers most of the standard techniques which, once mastered, should stand you in good stead to continue developing both skills and ideas.

ROUND

1 Mat

8in (20cm) diameter round base. Three sticks threaded through three.
Paired starting with tips.
Stake up and work a trac border.

2 Small Plant Holder

8in (20cm) diameter round base. Three sticks threaded through three.
Paired starting with tips.
Stake up, straight sides.
Upsett with three weavers starting with tips.
English Rand, approx 4in (10cm)
Wale.
Rod Border, three behind one.
Foot Border, three behind one.
Single rod twisted handles.

3 Small Basket with Bow Handle

10in (25cm) diameter round base. Three sticks threaded through three.
Paired starting with butts, then French rand starting with tips. Pair to finish base.
Stake up, straight sides.
Upsett with two sets of four weavers starting with butts.
French rand to 5in (13cm).
Place handle liners.
Wale.
Rod border, four-behind-two.
Single rope handle.

4 Small Log Basket

12in (30cm) diameter round base. Four sticks threaded through four.
Pair starting with butts. After 8in (20cm), start in two places with tips.
Stake up, flaired sides.
Upsett using three weavers on two sides starting with tips.
Double French rand to 12in (30cm).
Wale, starting on two sides.
Rod border, six-behind-two.
Foot-border, four-behind-two.
Two-rod twisted handles.

5 Round with Lid

14in (35cm) diameter round base. Four sticks threaded through four.
Pair starting with butts. After 8in (20cm), start in two places with tips.
Stake up straight sides.
Upsett using two sets of four weavers, starting with butts.
English rand, starting in front of two, behind one, in front of two. Four blocks.
Wale, starting both sides.
Rod border, four-behind-two, follow-on trac.
14in (35cm) diameter lid.
Pair starting with scallomed butts, French rand, wale.
Stake up for flange, wale and trac border.
Wale.
Stake up and work four-behind-two border.
Twisted loop at centre of lid.

OVAL

6 Shopping Basket

10 x 7in (25 x 18cm) oval base. Three threaded through seven.
Pair and reverse pair in blocks starting with tips.
Stake up minus one, flaired ends.
Upsett with two sets of four weavers, starting with butts.
Slew to 7in (18cm).
Place handle liners.
Wale starting two sides.
Rod border six-behind-two.
Twisted rope handle.

7 Doll's Cradle

12 x 8in (30 x 20cm) oval base. Four threaded through seven.
French rand, starting tips.
Stake up, flaired ends.
Upsett with two sets of four weavers, starting butts.
French rand.
Wale.
Pack one end.
Wale.
Plait border three x two.
Two small wrapped handles inserted into the sides.

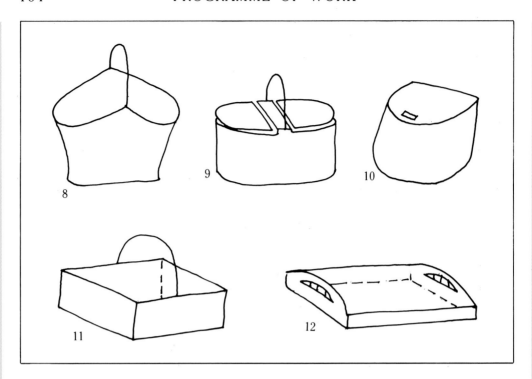

8 Shopping Basket

14 x 9in (35 x 23cm) oval base. Four threaded through eight.
French rand, starting butts.
Stake up.
Upsett using two sets of three weavers, starting with tips.
Pack both sides.
Wale.
Rolled handle and border in one.
Rolled foot border.

9 Double Lidded Basket

12 x 8in (30 x 20cm) oval base. Three threaded through seven.
French rand, starting butts.
Stake up, straight sides.
Upsett using two sets of four weavers, starting with butts.
French rand, in-front-of-two, behind-two, at handle position, using flat slat for handle liner.
Wale.
Rod border, four-behind-two.
Bridge.
Wrapped handle, two handle bows.
Two D-shaped lids with ties.
Hinges.

D-SHAPE
10 Fishing Basket

D-shaped base, 10 x 7in (25 x 18cm).
Scallomed front, staked up back.
Corner posts.
Wale starting with three tips at back, flowed out at front.
French rand.
Wale.
Rod border, four-behind-two.
D-shaped lid with notch and ties.
Hinges and fastening.

SQUARE
11 Small Shopping Basket

10 x 7in (25 x 18cm) randed square base.
English stake up.
Corner posts.
Upsett with two sets of three weavers, starting with tips.
Slew, starting in two places, up to 4in (10cm).
Wale.
Handle liners.
Rod border, five-behind-two, blunt corners.
Rope handle.

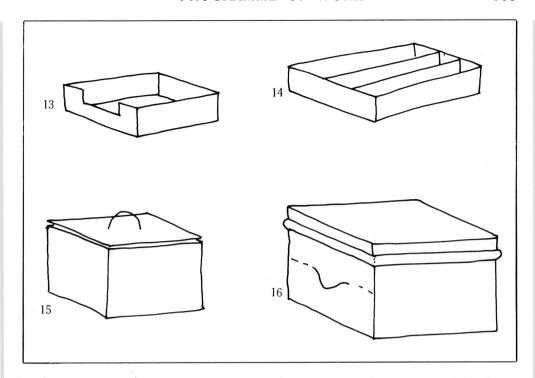

12 Tray

Square base, 18 x 12in (45 x 30cm) randed.
English stake up, blunt corners.
Upsett with two sets of three weavers, starting with butts.
Wale up to 2in (5cm).
Bye stake middle three end stakes.
Wale leaving an arch over the bye stakes.
Plait border, 3 x 3.

13 Desk tray

Square base, 15 x 11in (38 x 28cm), randed.
French stake up, corner posts, nine stakes each end.
Wale starting with two sets of three weavers, starting and finishing with tips.
Wale with three tips, starting on the left side of one end.
Bye stake notch with posts, same thickness as corners.
Butts the other end, bordering down four stakes to form notch.
Rand to 3½in (9cm).
Wale.
Rod border, four-behind-two, square corner, covering posts.
Ties at notch ends.

14 Cutlery Tray

Repeat instructions for desk tray without notch.
Make divisions for cutlery.

15 Case with Handle in Lid

Square base, 18 x 11in (45 x 28cm), randed.
French stake up, corner posts.
Wale with four sets of weavers, butt joins at centres.
French rand to 11in (28cm).
Wale.
Rod border, four-behind-two, exposed corner posts.
Lid to fit, single rod edges, wooden slats.
Two notches for fastenings.
Four-behind-two end borders with ties.
Hinges, fastening.
Small two-rod twisted handle on lid.

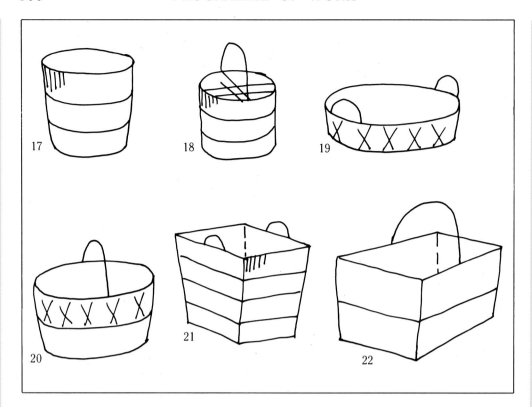

16 Trunk

Square base, 20 x 12in (50 x 30cm).
English stake up, corner posts.
Wale with four sets of weavers, butt joins at centres.
English rand to 12in (30cm).
Handles made from length of rope, woven in.
Trunk wale and border.
Trunk lid to fit.

FITCHING

17 Waste Paper Basket

Round hoop base, woven, 8in (20cm) diameter.
Scallomed stakes.
Fitched at 5in (13cm) and 8in (20cm).
Wale with two sets of four weavers, in-front-of-two, behind-two.
Plait border, 4 x 3.

18 Round Bottle Basket

Round hoop base, fitched, 8in (20cm) diameter.
Scallomed stakes.
Fitched at 4in (10cm) and 7in (18cm).
Wale with two sets of four rods, in-front-of-two, behind-two.
Rod border, six-behind-two.
Twisted rope handle.
Fitched divisions.

19 Layette Basket

Oval hoop base, woven, 14 x 8in (35 x 20cm).
Scallomed stakes.
Cross fitched at 4in (10cm).
Wale with two sets of four rods, in-front-of-two, behind-two.
Plait border, 5 x 2.
Two small attached handles.

20 Oval Shopping Basket

Oval hoop base, fitched slats, 14 x 8in (35 x 20cm).
Scallomed stakes.
Fitched at 4in (10cm).
Cross fitched at 7in (18cm).
Wale with two sets of four weavers, in-front-of-two, behind-two.
Rod border, six-behind-two.
Twisted rope handle.

21 Square Waste Paper Basket

Square hoop base, woven, 6 x 6in (15 x 15cm).
Scallomed stakes, scallomed corner posts.
Fitched four times at 2½in (6cm) intervals, starting at 3in (8cm) from base level.
Wale with two sets of four weavers, in-front-of-two, behind-two.
Plait border, 3 x 4, square corners.
Two small wrapped handles inserted into sides.

22 Shopping Basket

Square hoop base, woven, 12 x 8in (30 x 20cm).
Scallomed stakes, scallomed corner posts.
Fitched at 5in (13cm) and 9in (23cm) from base.
Wale with two sets of four weavers, in-front-of-two, behind-two.
Rod border, five-behind-two, square corners.
Twisted rope handle.

Chapter 11

DESIGNING

The design process is basically the same, regardless of the subject matter, and goes through the following stages.

1 Planning,
2 Problem Solving,
3 Evaluation.

It is a continuous process involving many skills, both manual and intellectual.

PLANNING

Skill and Experience

Take account of your level of skill and the limit of your experience in working with different techniques and materials. Do not try to tackle too much too soon; progress one step at a time.

Objectives

It is important to have clear objectives. You must decide which are the most important factors required of the finished product.
How long is it required to last?
How strong does it need to be?
Does it need weight or lightness?
How important is size?
Is colour important or colour fastness?
Is texture important, both visual and tactile?
Is it a 'one off' or will there be several?

Does it relate particularly well to one material rather than another?
Is one structural method more suitable than another?
Is fine detailing relevant?
Is it primarily to look at or to use?

Working Methods

You also need to decide on your working methods.
Are you adding to previous experience with variations and innovations, or trying something completely new?
Are you acquiring skill in a particular technique?
Do you prefer to make notes and work things out with sketches beforehand?
Do you like to work directly with the chosen material and experiment, trying out ideas as you go?

Preparation

You need to consider carefully the whole basket before you begin. Your preparation will need to take account of all parts of the basket.
You will need to prepare the right amount of material for use at one time.
The material will have to be sorted for your requirements.
You will have to allow the right amount of time to prepare the material for use.
You must consider the shape of the basket in terms of flow in order to calcu-

late the number of stakes.

Be prepared for handles, fastenings, lids and partitions: they must be an integral part of the design, not added on as an afterthought.

PROBLEM SOLVING

Problem solving is the 'nitty gritty' of the design process. The more experience you have, the more reference you have to help resolve problems, and the more complex the problems become. You need to be able to think objectively about your work to see where the problem is, how to remedy it and when to abandon it altogether, constantly comparing the result with the original criteria.

Materials

Is the material unfamiliar, of poor quality, insufficiently prepared or the wrong one for the task?

Is it too fine or too thick for the weave or in relation to the stakes?

Strength/Weight

Is the basic structure of the basket suitable for the purpose?
Is it too heavy or too flimsy?
Have you miscalculated the number of stakes?
Could you strengthen it or reduce it in any way?
Is the material used too thick, thin, soft or brittle?

Shape/Shaping

You need to develop an eye for form to enable you to make informed decisions about your work. You need to think about proportion, harmony and balance as well as function.

Shape out of control? Is it lack of skill, strength, care and concentration, or is the material wrong for the task? Can you redeem the situation by changing the weave or using stronger material?

Unable to achieve a shape? Are you using the right technique, the easiest method? Are you using the most appropriate number of stakes or weavers? Is the shape chosen the right one for the task?

Uneven siding? Have you got too many stakes or weavers, have they been selected carefully for similar thickness? Do you make enough use of a rule or rapping iron?

Colour

Use of colour need not imply a wide range. The simplicity of a well made basket in a single colour can show off detail and fine workmanship where multicolours could detract. Areas of one other colour can sometimes highlight use of different weaves to good effect.

Fresh natural materials have beautiful colours which invariably work well together, time toning them down to a range from gold to dark brown. Materials without intrinsic colour interest can benefit from the use of added coloured material or use of dyes and paint.

Use of colour is a skill in itself, and artists and scientists have spent lifetimes discovering how colours work for or against us. If you have a particular interest in working with colour, it is well worth the time spent studying other references.

Pattern and Texture

The diversity of texture and pattern that occurs in the straightforward structure of a basket by virtue of the techniques chosen gives added visual interest to the finished work. There are also many variations on the basic weaves which can be incorporated into the design, either as a feature or as an overall use of a mixture of textural interest. It is also possible to go beyond this into the realms of invention, using overlaid weavers, other materials and combinations of colours, to such an extent that the basket becomes an example of three dimensional woven textiles rather than purely a receptacle. Certain materials lend themselves to this style of work, in particular those that have great flexibility and are not resistant to dye, such as centre cane, as well as various fibres and even paper and card.

EVALUATION

The evaluation part of the design process is constant. You should continually be considering all aspects of what you can do. What works well, what could be used in another place or in another way. Assess to what extent you achieve what you set out to do and how you can improve on it or expand a particular idea. You can profit from your mistakes by changing your way of working. Alternatively, mistakes can be a useful way of setting you off on a new idea, experimenting and developing further in a way you had not anticipated.

Try working on a series of similar designs, with as many variations on a theme as you can think of. If you get stuck on a particular problem, leave it for a while and try something completely different.

Above all, aim for quality. You cannot achieve speed of working until you have developed the skills to produce work of a good standard. A simple and well made basket is infinitely better than a complex one poorly executed. 'Rustic charm' comes from the use of very basic, unrefined materials in a simple, straightforward way, *not* a badly proportioned, uneven basket with an unsecured handle or an ill-fitting lid.

A good design is suitable for its purpose in shape, size, weight, proportion, structure and materials. It also satisfies several senses; it looks and feels right and can sometimes smell and sound pleasant too.

GLOSSARY

Back The outside of the curve on a willow rod.

Bands Ties used to hold a border down.

Belly The inside of the curve of a willow rod.

Bolt A bundle of willow of one size prepared for sale.

Border The woven edge of a basket or lid.

Bottom Commonly used word for the base of a basket.

Bow Thick rod used to form the core of a handle.

Butt The thick end of a willow rod.

Bye Stake Extra stakes inserted after the upsett.

Clung Partially dried hedgerow material ready for use.

Cover Commonly used word for the lid of a basket.

Cram Off A stake or rod slyped and tapped into position where weaving away is difficult.

Fitch A two strand weave used to hold stakes into position after a space in the weaving.

Flow The degree by which the perimeter of the basket is greater at the top than the bottom.

Foot An extra border attached to the base of a basket.

Green Willow in its fresh state.

Grins Small gaps between the wrapping of a handle.

Kink Sharp bend in a willow rod.

Lapping Wrapping a core with a skein.

Leader Skein(s) or rod(s) used to secure the wrapping in skeinwork.

League Continuous rod through base and sides.

Liner Temporary rod or slat used to keep open a space for a handle in the siding.

Listing Extra skeins added to a lapped leader for a decorative finish.

Notch An opening in the side or lid of a basket.

Osier Basket willow.

Packing Weave used to build up one area of a basket.

Pairing A weave using two rods.

Pick Off Trimming off ends.

Piece In Joining a new weaver.

Prick Up Using a knife to open up a rod so that it will bend without cracking.

Rand A weave using one rod.

a) **Close** Randing rapped down after each round.

b) **Coarse** Randing not rapped down at all.

c) **Medium** Randing rapped down every few rounds.

d) **Prick** Randing begun by inserting the weavers into the siding.

Rod A whole willow shoot of one year's growth. Also a type of border.

Round A complete row of weaving.

Scallom A method of cutting the butt end of a willow rod.

Siding Commonly used term for the sides of a basket.

Skein Thin shaved strip cut from the outside of a willow rod.

Slath The base sticks tied together and opened out after the first few rows of weaving.

Slew Weave using two or more weavers together as one.

Slype A slanted cut.

Splint Thin piece of shaved wood used in certain types of basketry.

Stake Upright rod in the side of a basket to hold the weaving.

Stake Up Inserting the stakes into the base and preparing to weave the sides.

Stick Stout rod which forms the base or lid of a basket.

Stroke A complete movement repeated as part of a weave. (Equivalent to a single stitch in sewing or knitting.)

Tip The thin end of a willow rod.

Trac A type of border.

Trunk Cover A lid which fits over a basket.

Trunk Wale A thick wale on the side of a basket, usually to form a ledge for the lid to rest on.

Upsett The first few rows of waling after the side stakes have been pricked up.

Wale A weave using three or more weavers.

Weaver A rod that binds the stakes together.

Withy Another word for osier.

ACKNOWLEDGEMENTS

We would like to express our appreciation to the following for their practical help and encouragement:– Sheila Wynter, Bill Sykes, Meg Tapley, Stephen Byrne, Mark Baldwin and Dail Behennah. Special thanks are also due to Mr A. Coates of Gloucester and M. Gilles Bourgoine of Fayl-Billot, for their expertise as tutors, and to students both past and present. Above all, we are grateful for the unfailing support and encouragement of our husbands and families.

Photography by Gustav De Cozar with the exception of those from the Institute of Agricultural History and the Museum of English Rural Life, University of Reading, E. J. Wynter, Sally Goymer, Linda Lugenbill and Ben Braster.

BIBLIOGRAPHY

Many of these books are no longer in print, but they are usually available in (or through) libraries.

H.H. Bobart *Basketwork Through the Ages* (Oxford University Press, 1936) Historical

Germaine Brotherton *Rush and Leafcraft* (Batsford, 1977)

F.J. Christopher *Basketry* (Foyles) Useful all round book for beginners

Charles Crampton *Canework* (Dryad) The caneworker's manual

R. Duchesne, H. Ferrand, J. Thomas *La Vannerie* (J.B. Bailliere, 1981) Written in French, excellent diagrams

Norah Florence *Rushwork* (Bell, 1962)

Alistair Heseltine *Baskets and Basketmaking* (Shire Publications) Willow history, cultivation and processing – good diagrams and photographs

Phyllis Hosking *Basketmaking for Amateurs* (Bell, 1960) All-round book

A.G. Knock *Willow Basket Work* (Dryad, 1970) Good

Evelyn Legg *Country Baskets* (Mills and Boon, 1960) Useful information about hedgerow materials

Barbara Maynard *Modern Basketry from the Start* (Bell, 1973) Thorough on elementary techniques

Thomas Okey *The Art of Basketmaking* (Reprinted by the Basketmakers Association, 1986) Willow worker's manual – not many diagrams

Ed Rossbach *Baskets as Textile Art* (Studio Vista, 1974) Worldwide study of forms of basketry

Lyn Siler *The Basket Book* (Sterling, Blandford 1988) American style baskets using plaiting and framework techniques – excellent illustrations

Luther Weston Turner *The Basket Maker* (David Press, 1909) Good instructions on canework and the use of colour

Dorothy Wright *The Complete Book of Baskets and Basketry* (David & Charles, 1978) Wide range of techniques and recipes with good diagrams

INDEX